MW00881644

Special Operations Mental Toughness

The Invincible Mindset of Delta Force Operators, Navy SEALs, Army Rangers & Other Elite Warriors!

Author's Note

No classified information was used in the preparation of this book. All of the concepts, quotes, anecdotes, and other information contained within this book were derived from interviews and conversations with veterans of various special operations units; from selected special operations related books, training material, and websites; from interviews conducted by other authors; and from open-source media coverage of the various types of training and combat operations involving special operations units. The names of certain individuals cited in this book have been altered to protect their true identities.

Table of Contents

Introduction

The focus of this book is on the mindset, attitude, traits, and habits that enable special operators—the members of America's elite military units—to consistently perform with high levels of courage, competence, and precision in some of the most daunting and dangerous situations imaginable.

Most experts within the special operations community would likely agree with my assertion that the vast majority of special operators are not born with extraordinary talent and abilities; in fact, most of these men would describe themselves as being "for the most part, an average guy." The truth is that these men are, through continuous and incredibly challenging training, forged into some of the most capable and feared warriors ever to step onto a battlefield.

Much of the success achieved by the members of all of America's special operations units can be attributed to the individual traits and qualities they possess, such as mental toughness, self-confidence, self-control, resilience, and the ability to consistently perform well under pressure.

Most people would agree that these are some of the same qualities necessary to achieve a high-level of success in most aspects of one's personal and professional life; and many ambitious individuals spend much time and effort toward acquiring or enhancing them. The good news is that anyone, regardless of their age or physical capabilities, can develop the same levels of mental toughness and winning mindset possessed by the members of special operations units; and the purpose of this book is to help you do just that!

You should be aware of the fact that this book will not provide you with great detail about combat operations or the extensive training that transforms young men into special operators. It does, however, contain anecdotes, quotes, and information, which have been carefully selected for their effectiveness in illustrating certain aspects of the mindset, mental approach, and attitudes shared by members of America's special operations community. It also contains vignettes about several special operators who performed heroically during combat operations, and my hope is that these accounts will help illustrate the invincible mindset common to members of this very special breed of warriors.

The information contained in this book will aid anyone willing to work hard toward improving various aspects of their personal and professional lives. All that you need is the desire to achieve your goals and the awareness that in order to do so, it is necessary to assess your current situation, gain new perspectives, refocus, and when appropriate, implement some of the concepts, methods and techniques that are presented in this book.

Selection – The Rite of Passage

From the earliest civilizations, nations have formed military forces in order to defend their peoples and land against invading enemies and ensure the survival of their tribe or nation. Within these military forces, there have typically existed elite warrior units. These elite units were made up of those young men who had survived the most challenging tests of their courage and mental and physical toughness. Successfully completing these exceptionally demanding, and often dangerous, rites of passage would deem a young man worthy of being called a warrior. In addition to evaluating the courage and self-discipline of the prospective warriors, these rites of passage were designed to instill in them a fierce sense of patriotism, loyalty, obedience, and comradeship.

In the U.S. armed forces, the concept of the rite of passage continues to this day in the form of various SOF selection courses. Successfully completing one of these selection courses is only the beginning of a long journey a man must endure to become a member of an elite unit. This book will not address in detail any of the various training pipelines associated with SOF units. Instead, it will focus almost entirely on the topic of mental toughness and other traits associated with the strong-willed and confident mindset that men must exhibit in order to successfully complete a SOF selection course and subsequently perform well in a special operations unit.

This chapter will provide readers with a general overview of the intent, philosophies, and other aspects of these grueling rites of passage and it will help you gain a better understanding of the mindset and strength of character that enables members of these elite units to do what they do best—produce exceptional results in exceptionally challenging environments and situations.

The Purpose of SOF Selection Courses

There are two main goals that SOF selection courses are designed to attain. For obvious reasons, men who serve in SOF units must possess high levels of confidence, focus, discipline, and mental toughness. All selection courses serve the purpose of narrowing down the group of candidates and eliminating those who, in some way, lacked all the requisite attributes to succeed as special operators. By default, this relentless paring down of prospective operators will ensure that time, money, or valuable training resources are not wasted on individuals who would eventually prove not to be compatible with the duties associated with serving in a SOF unit.

Methods Vary

In his book *Lone Survivor*, retired Navy SEAL Marcus Luttrell explains in great detail the unbelievably harsh training young men must complete in order to become a member of the SEAL community. He shared that just before his BUD/S class was about to begin training, one of the instructors told the anxious and nervous young men, "You're going to hurt while you're here. That's our job: to induce pain—not permanent injury of course—but we need to make you hurt. That's a big part of becoming a SEAL. We need proof you can take the punishment. And the way out of that is mental, in your mind."

Each of the various SOF units utilizes slightly different methodologies in their selection courses. They all, however, share the commonality of the intensity with which they design the course in order to present the candidates with inconceivable amounts of physical and mental stress. Some of the tactics used in the courses include continuous and intense physical exercise, sleep deprivation, and constant evaluation by instructors. All of these very demanding selection courses require candidates to exhibit great amounts of mental toughness, determination, resilience, and the ability to think and act appropriately during stressful situations.

Training the candidates is NOT the main purpose of selection courses, but rather the objective is to push them to their physical and psychological limits in order to assess their ability to drive on when their body and brain are telling them to quit. This is the essence of all SOF selection courses—to identify men who can be counted on to remain focused and perform well during the most challenging, stressful and often, dangerous situations imaginable.

What Type of Man Are SOF Units Seeking?

Every SOF unit has a profile that lists the preferred moral, mental, and physical traits sought after in new candidates. Though the importance of these traits varies depending on the mission requirements of the various SOF units, there are some commonalities that these units are looking for in prospective special operators.

To illustrate these commonalities I will use material taken directly from the John F. Kennedy Special Warfare Center and School. This is the organization responsible for the selection and training of future members of the U.S. Army Special Forces (Green Berets); and although this material is focused on the Special Forces selection process, the tone and tenor of it is aligned with the core principles of all of the other SOF units in the U.S. military.

U.S. Army Special Forces Selection and Assessment

The Army's Special Forces Assessment and Selection course (SFAS) is "a sequential process of testing and evaluating soldiers with different measuring tools to determine which soldiers possess sufficient levels of the attributes required to be operationally successful."

Another important purpose of any special operations assessment and selection program is to identify individuals who are suited to perform a specific function or job within a SOF unit. In order to accomplish this, a valid set of selection criteria (attributes) and a relevant set of testing methods is needed. The logic behind assessment and selection is that once an individual is selected he can be trained to perform various tasks and skills required of a special operator.

Special Forces Assessment and Selection

The Army is looking for a certain type of man to fill the ranks of its Special Forces. The SFAS course and the Special Forces Qualification (Q Course) courses are exceptionally difficult, and like all SOF selection courses, they both have high attrition rates.

SFAS is designed to "identify a self-disciplined individual who is physically fit, intelligent, motivated, trainable, and possesses the attributes that will enable him to be a successful Special Forces soldier." This demanding selection course is based on four principles: "physically demanding, sleep deprivation, induced stress, and increasing performance objectives." These four principles, to various degrees, are inherent to all Special Forces missions.

SFAS attempts to capture a soldier's profile by first administering a series of mental, learning, and personality tests, and secondly by processing the soldier through a series of field-related assessment activities. In other words, SFAS exists to screen candidates to see if they are worthy of beginning the long and arduous training associated with becoming a member of the Special Forces; its sole purpose is to identify and select the strong and capable, while eliminating candidates that are in one way or another not suited for service in a Special Forces unit.

The 24 day course takes place at the Col. Nick Rowe Special Forces Training Facility in Camp MacKall, North Carolina. Typical elements of the SFAS course include:

- Day and night marches of varying lengths with a 50lb backpack. As an added stressor, the duration of these marches is not revealed to the candidates.
- Timed runs—with or without packs
- Obstacle courses designed to test fitness and stamina, but also to weed out candidates with a fear of heights or enclosed spaces
- Orienteering, land navigation, and field-craft exercises test the candidate's ability to traverse terrain utilizing map and compass.
- Situation and Reaction Exercises are designed to evaluate the candidates' ability to solve complex problems while mentally and physically exhausted.
- Team Cooperation Exercises test the candidates' ability to work together and accomplish a common goal. Being able to

work as a part of a team while under pressure is an important attribute of a Special Forces soldier.

Throughout the course the candidates are purposefully deprived of sleep and in a state of heightened mental strain. By the second week of the course, approximately half of the beginning candidates will have either quit or been eliminated from the course. Those who complete the course undergo a final evaluation by the instructors and training cadre; and those who show the sought after qualities and attributes are allowed the opportunity to attend the Special Forces Qualification course.

Many men have completed SFAS, but in the final analysis were found to be lacking in some way by the review board. This should illustrate that the leaders of SOF units are looking for much more than physical strength and endurance from prospective special operators. They have learned over time that any number of intangible and difficult-to-define traits and habits are the critical ingredients that enable a man to successfully serve in a special operations unit.

The 13 Attributes of an Army Special Forces Soldier

After evaluating the results of several SFAS courses and doing a very detailed review of the men that passed or failed the course, the Special Forces leaders were able to identify and define thirteen attributes that are now deemed essential for a Special Forces soldier. As you'll see, this list contains some attributes, such as physical fitness, that are obvious requirements for a special operator. It also contains some that fall into the "intangible and difficult-to-define" category mentioned previously. Listed below are the 13 attributes associated with serving as a Special Forces soldier:

1. Physical Fitness: Displays acceptable levels of muscular strength and endurance, stamina, and motor coordination.

2. Motivation: Persists at accomplishing tasks. Takes the initiative to participate in or complete a task without hesitation or delay.

3. Teamwork: Capable of working effectively in a small group environment.

4. Stability: Able to control emotions (e.g. fear, anger, happiness, frustration) in order to remain effective and efficient in attainment of the objective. Composure under stress—does not become unnecessarily excited under pressure.

5. Trustworthiness: Demonstrates integrity and honesty in all actions and words.

6. Accountability: Able to follow instructions, keep track of equipment, and be responsible for himself. Shows awareness of and concern for safety rules and restrictions.

7. Intelligence: Comprehends and applies concepts. Can recognize and analyze the components of a problem and develop courses of action to solve the problem.

8. Maturity: Recognizes and demonstrates appropriate behavior for any given situation.

9. Communication: Relays essential information in a clear and logical manner in order to accomplish the mission.

10. Judgement: Considers all known facts in order to make logical decisions when choosing among alternative solutions.

11. Influence: Able to persuade team members to accomplish their common goal.

12. Decisiveness: Capable of implementing a plan and executing a course of action in a firm, prompt, and positive manner. Will not change his decision without good cause.

13. Responsibility: Accomplishes leadership task, including the development and implementation of plans and supervision of others. Ensures the health and welfare of all team members. Completes tasks in accordance with established mission constraints.

I want to emphasize once again that although the 13 attributes listed above are associated with the Army's SFAS program, I'm confident that most, if not all, senior leaders within other SOF units would generally agree that these attributes are also what they are seeking in candidates for their respective units.

Why Men Quit Selection Courses

In his book *Always Faithful, Always Forward: The Forging of a Special Operations Marine*, retired Navy SEAL Dick Couch had this to say about the rites of passage associated with America's special operations community: "Few processes in our culture, military or otherwise, lay bare the physical, psychological, and emotional worth of an individual as do our SOF selection programs. It is a rendering for the essentials of the human spirit."

Couch's thoughts are supported by the high attrition rates of all SOF selection courses. Many of these men fail because they are unable to meet certain physical, academic, or moral standards. However, the main reason candidates fail selection is because they quit.

For reasons known only to them, these men have lost the confidence and desire they once had for joining a SOF unit. As they let negative thoughts dominate their minds, they typically begin to slow down during graded events and their class standing suffers. Once they allow these obstacles to get the better of them, they simply give in to their negative thoughts and give up the fight.

The Virus

During a conversation with a former member of the U.S. Army's Delta Force, I asked for his thoughts on why so many apparently qualified and motivated men ultimately quit SOF selection courses. His thoughts concurred with the notion that most of these men simply surrendered to negative thoughts and a feeling of hopelessness, both of which were magnified by the fact that, in most instances, they had been worn down physically and were experiencing levels of fatigue and discomfort far higher than they'd ever previously experienced.

This retired special operator referred to this self-defeating type of thinking as "the virus." He began to use this term because over the course of many years of being associated with and observing various SOF selection courses, he realized that when a man begins to have negative thoughts and doubts during selection, if these thoughts are not quickly dismissed or negated by the candidate, they will spread as rapidly inside of his mind as an actual viral infection does in a human body if left untreated.

All the SOF veterans I have spoken with agree that once the "virus of negativity and self-pity" takes over a man's mind, they literally talk themselves into believing that their only option is to quit the selection course.

The End Product

In the final analysis, a SOF selection course identifies men that possess the raw aptitude and traits to serve as a special operator. Once selection is completed, these men continue through the qualification pipeline and participate in extensive follow-on training. Even after a SOF selection course is over, selection never really ends! This concept is validated by the fact that some men who manage to successfully complete one of the various SOF selection courses will still, for various reasons, be dismissed from the training pipeline and fall short of becoming a fully-vetted and qualified special operator.

As you can see, prospective special operators are put through an incredibly difficult rite of passage that calls for an extraordinary amount of mental toughness, self-discipline, and resilience. Although most of these men possess these qualities when they begin their respective selection courses, it is during these courses that they are required to demonstrate high tolerances for pain, discomfort, and uncertainty. Those who are able to persevere, while their peers are quitting, show that they possess the mental fortitude to successfully and effectively function in the environments and situations that members of SOF units invariably operate in.

If you study and reflect upon some of the traits that SOF units are in search of, and how candidates undergoing selection courses portray them, you'll discover that you can in fact develop the same high-level of mental toughness and resolve necessary for setting and achieving challenging goals in your personal or professional life.

The Special Operator Mindset

Throughout my many years of military service, I maintained a notebook in which I recorded random thoughts and ideas concerning the topic of mental toughness and other individual qualities related to the members of various special operations units. Over time, I had created a large collection of notes that listed some of the dominant personality traits and attitudes that I had observed in many special operators from various SOF units. I have distilled these notes so they can help you better understand what I feel are some of the major aspects of the mindset shared by the members of America's most elite military units.

Confidence in Their Training

Later in this book you will be introduced to an important ingredient of mental toughness: Confidence. This key ingredient is attained via several sources, one of which is the training that special operators receive.

From the outset of a SOF selection course, prospective special operators undergo such rigorous challenges, testing, and evaluation, that at its conclusion they know they have succeeded in passing a rite of passage that most men cannot. Once the extensive follow-on operator training courses and programs are completed, newly minted special operators feel fully prepared to accomplish any mission or task assigned to them. They believe in their training and the skills they've acquired and this belief is the foundation in the development of their self-confidence.

A Winning Mentality

Competitiveness is a common characteristic possessed by special operators. A strong desire to win propels candidates to maintain focus and persevere throughout the incredibly difficult training of selection courses, and this competitive nature continues once special operators join their units. Their confidence is such that they believe they can accomplish any assignment better even than their more experienced teammates.

Positive Self-talk

Most successful special operators are able to utilize positive self-talk as a means to eliminate doubt and bolster confidence when they face difficult, stressful situations. We all engage in some form of self-talk almost continuously throughout the day. It is very important to ensure that this self-talk is of a positive nature rather than negative.

Control Doubts

Doubt destroys confidence, and confidence is paramount to success. It is important that you learn to take measures when you notice doubt setting in in order to combat it. Special operators are trained to refocus their attention to positive thoughts and to focus on visualizing the immediate tasks that need to be performed. This leads to a state of mind more conducive to mission accomplishment and success.

Anticipate Success

Visualization is a technique used by most special operators prior to engaging in an event or during the pursuit of a goal. It entails a mental rehearsal of the various tasks or maneuvers that will be carried out during a mission or exercise.

Project Confidence

Most special operators are optimists by nature, and this enables them to see opportunities where others might see obstacles and challenges too difficult to overcome. Fueling this optimism is the extensive training and personal development that all special operators undergo, which produces in them an unshakeable confidence in their abilities to overcome any challenge, big or small.

Whatever the task or mission at hand, special operators approach it with a very positive, optimistic attitude all the while sure of their training and fully confident in their upcoming successful mission accomplishment.

Develop Strategies and Game Plans

Special operators understand the necessity of devising a detailed plan for any action that they will have to take during a mission. The need to be able to control as many factors in any given situation is of utmost importance. As you can imagine, all special operators are expected to think on their feet in order to adjust plans as changes on the battlefield dictate.

Standard Operating Procedures (SOPs) for military units, which encompass the tactical and technical procedures carried out by SOF teams, have been developed by consolidating the vast array of individual and collective experiences of veteran special operators throughout their careers. These SOPs are memorized and practiced relentlessly by every member of a SOF unit, and they cover everything from the most complex tactics to the minutiae of loading the different weapons the teams use.

This amount of rehearsal prior to a mission allows the members of SOF units to be confident in the plan of attack and to react accordingly when unexpected events occur. It is a well-known fact that no battle plan is perfect, and a unit will inevitably have to adjust their mission plan—regardless how sound and detailed—due to the many obstacles that will undoubtedly arise once the battle begins.

It is imperative that operators remain mentally flexible and ready to respond with timely decisions to counter them. In fact, they practice this skill continuously during training so they can maintain and refine their ability to cope with the unexpected, no matter what it is, and remain focused on the most important thing: successful accomplishment of the assigned mission. Knowing that they have acquired this skill is in itself a confidence builder and a significant part of the mental toughness associated with men serving in SOF units.

Exercise Patience

Although an accurate description of special operators is that of physically strong, mentally tough men of action, it must be made clear that there are times when the ability to exercise a high degree of patience is critical. Regardless of the activity a special operator is undertaking, he must have the ability to sense when being patient is the best course of action. This will help him avoid situations where he might react too quickly or in a manner that provides the enemy with an advantage or otherwise endangers the successful accomplishment of the mission or assigned tasks.

Continuous Testing

For special operators the test is never over! The selection course is only the beginning of a never ending series of tests. Once they have successfully completed their initial training and report to their units, they will have to prove to themselves as well as to their teammates that they can be depended on to execute flawlessly when lives are on the line.

These exceptional warriors thrive in combat operations and in other situations associated with extreme danger because their ability to perform is constantly being tested and evaluated in some way. So the question many ask is: Why do they subject themselves to such high levels of stress and hardship?

A psychologist working in the special operations community deduced that it is because of their innate desire to excel and achieve objectives deemed almost impossible to attain. Furthermore, this psychologist states that this need to outperform can be linked to a certain level of excitement and the surge of adrenaline that results from executing tasks at the highest levels. These same spikes in adrenaline and other hormones experienced by extreme athletes and other military personnel are also evident in Wall Street stock traders, business executives, surgeons, and even salesmen closing a deal. It seems that high achievers, and special operators alike, thrive in significantly challenging and stressful situations!

Special operators have countless other positive attributes and personality traits, but those listed above are what I feel are the main factors that result in the mental toughness, confidence, and competence associated with these warriors.

You should reflect upon the traits and qualities of special operators mentioned in this chapter. Think about some of the successful people you have encountered in your life. The ones you should strive to emulate are those who demonstrate the competitive nature as well as the relentless quest for excellence associated with the members of special operations units.

Lieutenant Michael P. Murphy

U.S. Navy SEAL

On the night of June 27, 2005, Lt. Michael P. Murphy boarded a Chinook helicopter with his SEAL team as part of an operation designed to stop insurgents from disrupting the upcoming national elections in Afghanistan. Lieutenant Murphy and his teammates—Petty Officers Marcus Luttrel, Danny Dietz, and Matt Axelson—were assigned the mission to infiltrate the Hindu-Kush mountains, locate, and capture or eliminate Ahmad Shah, the leader of a terrorist guerrilla group operating near the Pakistani border.

The four-man team hiked for hours through the snow covered mountains toward their observation site. The fog deemed the observation site ineffective, so the team decided to move to a second location. When they arrived at a clearing suitable for observation of the suspected location of their target, they concealed themselves behind rocks, tree stumps, and tree branches. Soon after, two Afghan goat-herders happened upon their position. Finding no evidence that the goat-herders were insurgents, unable to establish communications with their command, and not willing to violate the rules of engagement, the team opted to let them go.

Although the SEALs feared the goat-herders would inform the Taliban of their presence, they decided to move to another location and continue the mission. Their fears proved true and a short while later they were ambushed deep in the mountains of Afghanistan.

Running, falling, and hurling themselves down the mountain, the SEAL team attempted to reach the village below in order to find cover and a place to make a stand against the enemy forces. Stopping only to reload, reassess, and attempt communications, the SEAL team fought on as a barrage of AK-47 fire, rocket-propelled grenades, and mortar rounds incessantly assailed them.

Under unyielding pressure from Shah's men and still unable to establish communications, they had no choice but to continue their perilous descent. Petty Officer Dietz was killed; the remaining 3 were wounded by enemy fire as well as from injuries sustained from falling and jumping hundreds of feet down the rocky slope.

Knowing that their situation was dire at best, Murphy understood that their best chance of survival would be to establish communications to request support. Radio communication unavailable from their position, Murphy knew that using his satellite phone was their only option; however, Murphy had to expose himself to enemy fire in order to reach a high enough position to get a signal.

With AK-47 bullets ricocheting around him, Murphy said, "My men are taking heavy fire ... we're getting picked apart. My guys are dying out here ... we need help." He was hit in the back by an AK-47 round, which knocked his phone and rifle out of his hands. Fatally wounded, he managed to retrieve both, complete the call for rescue, and continue to fight. Murphy succumbed to his wounds shortly thereafter. Thanks to his call for rescue, Petty Officer Marcus Luttrell was eventually located and rescued.

On October 27, 2007, Lieutenant Michael P. Murphy was posthumously awarded the Medal of Honor, America's highest award for battlefield courage.

CITATION:

For conspicuous gallantry and intrepidity at the risk of his life above and beyond the call of duty as a member of SEAL Deliver Vehicle Team ONE and the leader of a special reconnaissance element with Naval Special Warfare Task Unit Afghanistan on 27 and 28 June 2005. While leading a mission to locate a high-level anti-coalition militia leader, Lieutenant Murphy demonstrated extraordinary heroism in the face of grave danger in the vicinity of Asadabad, Konar Province, Afghanistan. On 28 June 2005, operating in an extremely rugged enemy-controlled area, Lieutenant Murphy's team was discovered by anti-coalition militia sympathizers, who revealed their position to Taliban fighters. As a result, between 30 and 40 enemy fighters besieged his four-member team. Demonstrating exceptional resolve, Lieutenant Murphy valiantly led his men in engaging the large enemy force. The ensuing fierce firefight resulted in numerous enemy casualties, as well as the wounding of all four members of the team. Ignoring his own wounds and demonstrating exceptional composure, Lieutenant Murphy continued to lead and encourage his men. When the primary communicator fell mortally wounded, Lieutenant Murphy repeatedly attempted to call for assistance for his beleaguered teammates. Realizing the impossibility of communicating in the extreme terrain, and in the face of almost certain death, he fought his way into open terrain to gain a better position to transmit a call. This deliberate, heroic act deprived him of cover, exposing him to direct enemy fire. Finally achieving contact with his headquarters, Lieutenant Murphy maintained his exposed position while he provided his location and requested immediate support for his team. In his final act of bravery, he continued to engage the enemy until he was mortally wounded, gallantly giving his life for his country and for the cause of freedom. By his selfless leadership, courageous actions, and extraordinary devotion to duty, Lieutenant Murphy reflected great credit upon himself and upheld the highest traditions of the United States Naval Service.

Mental Toughness

All U.S. Special Operations Forces undergo rigorous selection and training programs that are designed to push men past their perceived physical and mental limitations. Although training methods and requirements differ among SOF units, their ultimate goal is to separate the strong from the weak in order to ensure that only the most committed men become members of their respective units. The optimal group of selectees is achieved by setting candidates in a constant state of mental turmoil, causing their minds to constantly battle within as they face the decision to either "quit" or "stay" multiple times per day.

Aside from identifying those capable of serving as a special operator, the training is also designed to produce a warrior who is supremely confident in his abilities and, by default, those of his teammates. Any special operator will agree that of all the individual traits and qualities required of him and his teammates, there is one that stands out as the single most critical factor in determining whether or not a man can pass a special operations selection course and become an effective member of a SOF unit: Mental toughness.

Possessing an extraordinary level of mental toughness is the foundation upon which a special operator is selected and trained. This mental toughness enables him to achieve success when the odds are stacked against him. It is the trait that causes him to demonstrate a refuse-to-lose mindset, and it is the underpinning of the unswerving loyalty and dedication that he has toward his teammates.

A high-level of mental toughness is also associated with success and high-achievement in many other non-military professions and environments. This chapter is designed to help you understand more about this trait and ways that you can develop it relative to your own life and any goals you may want to achieve.

What Is Mental Toughness?

The topic of mental toughness has been debated for decades, and to the best of my knowledge there is still not a standard, widely accepted definition for the term. It is used by military trainers, coaches of all types, business leaders, and sports psychologists. From an athletic perspective, the term is used to describe an athlete that possesses the ability to remain focused and perform well under very stressful circumstances. Military leaders use it to describe the traits necessary to enable a warrior to remain calm in extremely dangerous, life threatening situations, and to make the appropriate decisions or perform the tasks required to accomplish the mission.

In his book *The Art of Mental Training*, author and former Marine Corps aviator D.C. Gonzalez said this about the often difficult to quantify trait of mental toughness:

> *I need you to recall an occasion when you performed at your best—and then remember a time when you were at your worst. Now when you look at those two performances, I want you to be honest with yourself and ask, what made the most difference between the two? Could it have been your mental state that made the most difference? . . . And that's the important point: no matter what your game is, or what the challenge is, the difference between great performances and average performances is mostly mental. Once you reach a certain level of skill, it's your mental skills that start making all the difference. The better they are, the better you will become—and the better your results will be.*

The famous sports psychologist Dr. Jim Loehr of the Human Performance Institute defined mental toughness as follows:

> *Mental toughness is the ability to consistently perform towards the upper range of your talent and skill regardless of competitive circumstances. It is all about improving your mind so that it's always on your side; not*

sometimes helping you nor working against you as we all know it's quite capable of doing.

Special Operators Talk about Mental Toughness

I thought it would be beneficial to include some quotes and comments made by several special operators on the topic of mental toughness. While each of them has his own personality and way of expressing his thoughts on the topic, I think you'll agree that their comments all reflect the "refuse to lose" and "never give up" mentality that is instilled in special operators from the very first day of their training:

> *"In my opinion, mental toughness is the ability to remain calm when others are overcome by fear or panic, and being able to do whatever needs to be done to win."*

> *"Mental toughness is not letting anyone or anything break you."*

> *"As a former Pararescueman, I believe that mental toughness is the ability to stay focused and overcome anything that might degrade your ability to achieve the mission. It is the ability to adapt and perform well under the worst conditions possible."*

"No matter what happens, I simply refuse to lose. To me, it's really that simple. I approach anything thought to be difficult with an attitude of 'I'll do this or die trying.'"

"It means that whenever most people would make excuses why something can't be done, I focus on finding a way to get it done."

"Mental toughness is the belief that, as long as I'm breathing and my brain is functioning, I have the ability to succeed at any given task."

"During my service in a Ranger unit, I learned that mental toughness is a man's ability to defeat the voice in his mind that is telling him to quit."

"I've seen a lot of mentally tough guys during my time in the Teams, and the common trait they possess is that they all believe that adversity brings out the best in them and that there's always a way to win."

"The ability to stay focused when ordinary men would buckle under the pressure or be consumed by fear."

"Mental toughness is doing whatever is necessary to accomplish the mission."

"You simply cannot be a Navy SEAL without being mentally tough. You wouldn't make it through BUD/S, and you certainly wouldn't be able to operate in combat if you weren't. SEALs must have the mental ability to block out physical pain and fear, while remaining highly focused on whatever is required to achieve victory."

"I was never able to shake my fear of heights and never enjoyed jumping out of an airplane at twenty thousand feet, yet I did so hundreds of times over my twenty-year career. I simply decided that my desire to serve in the Special Forces was stronger than the fear I felt toward jumping. The men who wear the Green Beret aren't immune from fear; they simply refuse to let it affect them in a negative way. That's what mental toughness means to me."

Do You Know Someone Who Is Mentally Tough?

Think for a moment of a person who is known for being mentally tough. Odds are that this person has established a reputation for achieving consistently superior results under a wide range of conditions or in various types of situations involving stress, pressure, and risk. He or she likely maintains a positive attitude and approach to achieving his or her goals, and remains focused on winning despite numerous distractions and changing circumstances. Resilience and enthusiasm even in the face of setbacks, disappointing results, and mistakes, as well as the ability to remain focused on accomplishing stated goals or objectives, are all probably qualities this person exemplifies.

While I have known many mentally tough operators from various SOF units, I must say that some of the most mentally tough people I have ever met were not in the military. Meeting and knowing some of these people caused me to understand that mental toughness was not a quality exclusive to special operators. I learned, through observation and interaction with these people, that some of the most physically frail individuals are often as mentally tough as any special operator is—maybe even more so!

I've seen people battle cancer for years, enduring countless sessions of chemotherapy, knowing all the while that their chances of survival were low, yet they kept fighting. I had a friend who was struck by throat cancer in his early 40s. He suffered through two long years of chemo and radiation treatments to no avail. Throughout his battle with cancer, he exhibited a level of determination and "fire in the gut" that was impressive and humbling at the same time. I don't think he ever stopped believing that he would ultimately beat the disease, and he remained upbeat and positive right up until the very moment he left this life. He was never in the military, but I can tell you without reservation that he had the type of mental toughness that special operators need and that you likely want to develop.

The point I am trying to convey is that, while all special operators are mentally tough, one does not have to serve in the military to develop this valuable attribute. It is not an innate quality that only some lucky few possess. Through the development or improvement of certain skills—self-discipline, character, resilience, focus, etc.—mental toughness is a quality that you can develop, hone, and master with time, work, and determination. It is what ultimately results of a relentless effort toward improvement in all aspects of a persons' life.

Senior Airman Jason D. Cunningham
Air Force Pararescueman

On March 4, 2002, in the snowy mountains of the Paktia Province in Afghanistan, Navy SEAL Petty Officer 1st Class Neil Roberts was thrown off a Chinook helicopter during a drop-off maneuver. Roberts' team reentered the area where he had fallen, but were immediately met with heavy enemy fire. Senior Airman Jason D. Cunningham, an Air Force Pararescueman on his first combat mission was assigned as the medic for a quick reaction force that would attempt to reinforce the team that was already on the mountain and engaged with enemy forces.

The situation on the mountain was dire; Roberts had been captured and killed and the rest of his team was in an intense battle for their lives. As the helicopter carrying Cunningham neared the enemy position, it was struck by rocket-propelled grenades and small arm fire disabling it and forcing a crash landing. Cunningham immediately began to treat the many wounded as the Rangers onboard ran out to engage the enemy.

Realizing how dangerous their position was, Cunningham and the other medics decided to move their patients to a more secure location. They were immediately barraged by mortar rounds that landed as close as 50 feet away from them. While extracting and moving his patients from the wreckage of the helicopter to the other location,

Cunningham crossed the line of fire seven times. Soon thereafter, their second location also became compromised, and Cunningham and the other medics had to once again move the wounded.

One of the other medics was shot in the abdomen as they moved patients to the third location. A short while later Cunningham received a mortal wound to his abdomen, which shattered his liver and caused internal bleeding. Despite his injuries, Cunningham continued directing the efforts to move the wounded to safety. His injuries were severe and he bled to death on the mountain top as they awaited evacuation.

Two hours after his death a helicopter finally arrived to evacuate the ten wounded soldiers that Cunningham fought so hard to protect.

For his exceptional courage under fire, Senior Airman Jason D. Cunningham was posthumously awarded the Air Force Cross on September 13th, 2002.

CITATION:

For extraordinary heroism in military operations against an opposing armed force while serving as a Pararescueman of the 38th Rescue Squadron, 247th Operations Group, in action near the village of Marzak in the Paktia Province of Afghanistan on 4 March 2002. On that proud day, Airman Cunningham was the primary Air Force Combat Search and Rescue medic assigned to a Quick Reaction Force tasked to recover two American servicemen evading capture in austere terrain occupied by massed Al Qaida and Taliban forces. Shortly before landing, his MH-47E helicopter received accurate rocket-propelled grenade and small arms fire, severely disabling the aircraft and causing it to crash land. The assault force formed a hasty defense and immediately suffered three fatalities and five critical casualties. Despite effective enemy fire, and at great risk to his own life, Airman Cunningham remained in the burning fuselage of the aircraft in order to treat the wounded. As he moved his patients to a more secure location, mortar rounds began to impact within fifty feet of his position. Disregarding this extreme danger, he continued the movement and exposed himself to enemy fire on seven separate occasions. When the second casualty collection point was also compromised, in a display of uncommon valor and gallantry, Airman Cunningham braved an intense small arms and rocket-propelled grenade attack while repositioning the critically wounded to a third collection point. Even after he was mortally wounded and quickly deteriorating, he continued to direct patient movement and transferred care to another medic. In the end, his distinct efforts led to the successful delivery of ten gravely wounded Americans to life-saving medical treatment. Through his extraordinary heroism, superb airmanship, aggressiveness in the face of the enemy, and in the dedication of his service to his country, Senior Airman Cunningham reflected the highest credit upon himself and the United States Air Force.

Developing Mental Toughness

Can Mental Toughness Be Taught?

I believe that mental toughness can be taught, and the results of numerous research studies validate my belief. While it is apparent that some individuals have higher levels of mental toughness as a result of their childhood experiences—sports, economic and social factors, parental guidance, etc.—it does appear that this quality can be cultivated and developed through specific training and education.

Because of the real-world demands placed on special operations forces, it is critical that members of such units be pushed to their physical limitations in order to replicate the stress levels associated with combat situations. This type of physical rigor is also useful for athletes and for those engaged in activities that include a high level of physical exertion or effort. But there are also many professions, activities, and environments in which physical exertion and the necessity for physical strength and fitness are limited or even nonexistent, yet still require a great amount of mental toughness in order to perform at optimal levels.

Physicians, trial attorneys, stock traders, airline pilots, business owners, and entrepreneurs are some examples of professions in which physical prowess is of little consequence, yet a person's success can often be directly impacted by the presence or absence of mental toughness. Additionally, people involved in various "personal battles"—such as situations at work; dealing with family or personal relationship problems; coping with health issues, drug addiction, alcoholism, obesity—need a great amount of mental toughness in order to push past their limitations, deal with the challenges facing them, and follow whatever steps are necessary to achieve their goals.

Define What Mental Toughness Means for You

For men aspiring to become members of special operations units, mental toughness is the ability to remain focused and motivated throughout the various stages and events associated with a selection course. Once selected into their respective units, mental toughness becomes even more important as these warriors routinely participate in very dangerous, mentally and physically demanding training that requires them to perform at near peak output for very long periods of time, often with infrequent periods of rest and recovery. And, of course, in today's very troubled world, there's a near certainty that most, if not all, current and future special operators will participate in frequent deployments to combat zones.

For you, demonstrations of mental toughness may mean:

- Waking up an hour or more earlier each day so you can meditate, pray, read, or workout before you go to work or school.

- Spending an extra hour per day interacting with your spouse, children, friends, etc.

- Spending one hour per day learning a skill that you desire to become competent at.

- Going one month without missing a workout

- Going one week without eating processed or otherwise unhealthy foods

- Getting through an entire month without consuming alcohol

- Planning and accomplishing work-related goals and tasks for an entire week

Whatever it is that you would like to do that would require you to demonstrate mental toughness, make sure that you write it down and clearly define what you want to achieve. Mental toughness is an abstract quality that is best developed by associating planned actions to specific and measurable goals. In other words, to develop mental toughness, you actually have to do something—you have to willfully and deliberately take action toward accomplishing goals and achieving results.

Get Comfortable Being Uncomfortable

If you were able to speak with a member of one of America's SOF units on the topic of developing mental toughness, he would undoubtedly agree that a major factor in an individual's ability to become mentally tough is whether or not he or she is able to "get comfortable being uncomfortable."

Why is this so important? It's because whatever it is that you want to achieve in life (assuming that you've set challenging goals), ultimately your success will depend upon your ability to persevere and push through situations or periods of time that bring forth various forms of discomfort, stress, anxiety, friction, self-doubt, and in some instances, actual physical pain.

This really is the key to building mental toughness. You cannot simply wake up one morning and declare that because you desire to be mentally tough, you now actually possess this trait. The special operators I know who served as instructors within SOF units all believe that it takes time to develop a high-level of mental toughness and that a person needs to work at it every single day in a variety of ways.

How to Develop Mental Toughness

The following are some examples of steps you can take to begin developing or enhancing your level of mental toughness.

1. Take Action

One of the easiest things you can do in order to start your path toward developing mental toughness is to simply "decide." Once you've made the decision, all you have to do is "something." Even the smallest step is a step closer to your goal. The longer you wait to begin, the longer it will take you to reach your objective. You will find that once you've taken that first step, no matter how small, all the following steps come much easier.

At some point in their lives, every special operator decided to step up and initiate the process of entering their respective selection course. For some, this decision came after only a brief period of deliberation, while others had constantly thought about making this move for several years. The bottom line is that, ultimately, they all took action and did whatever was necessary to begin the rite of passage that stood between them and admission to a special operations unit.

Whether your ultimate goal is to start exercising, become faster, increase muscle mass, obtain a college degree, become certified in a new skill, write a book, win a promotion at work, or perhaps even change careers, you must take the first step that begins the journey that leads to your definition of success. Don't sit idle and make excuses, don't talk yourself out of working toward achieving what you want. The best way to achieve your goal is to simply get started, so sit back and reflect on what you need to do and take action!

2. Focus on Small Victories

Developing mental toughness is always associated with establishing effective personal habits. It's literally about doing the things you know you're supposed to do (or avoiding things you know you should not do) on a more consistent basis. It's about your willingness to become and remain motivated to establish and follow a daily schedule of actions and tasks that will yield the results you're seeking.

Mental toughness is best developed by achieving "small victories" on a day-by-day basis. For example, if you desire to lose weight, instead of vowing to eat properly for the next 90 days, simply resolve to attack your weight-loss goal one meal at a time. If you eat a good breakfast, you will likely be motivated to do the same when it is time for lunch. After eating well for the first two meals of the day, it will be much easier to maintain your momentum and stay disciplined during your evening meal. If you can manage to eat well for an entire day, this will probably enable you to stay focused and motivated throughout the following day; and if you can eat well throughout the entire second day, you'll have all the more reason to stay the course during the third day, and so forth.

There's a saying that's popular in the special operations community regarding how one should approach large and seemingly impossible tasks. In this example, the question posed is: "How do you eat an elephant?" The appropriate answer is "One bite at a time!" This approach is often used by candidates undergoing a SOF selection course. Instead of contemplating many more months or weeks of grueling tests before they graduate the course and achieve their goal of joining a SOF unit, they instead simply focus on the task they are doing at the time and nothing else.

A Navy SEAL once told me that when he was going through BUD/S he focused on surviving until the next meal. He knew that on almost all training days his class would run to the chow hall at fairly predictable times, and that the training day was almost always concluded soon after the evening meal. He told me that he literally got through BUD/S by focusing on the 4-5 hour periods of time (and the training evolutions conducted during these periods) between meals and nothing else.

So, establish a daily schedule that causes you to take actions at a specific time and in a measurable way. Develop a routine and stick to it so you can begin to achieve small victories throughout each day. Focus on your behavior and the results will follow!

3. Set Goals

A proven method to establish habits that lead to small victories is setting goals. It is beyond debate that establishing goals and embedding them in the subconscious mind results in a more focused, determined, and persistent individual. In other words, when you consciously reflect upon goals you want to achieve, write them down, and review them on a daily basis, they begin to occupy a prominent position in your subconscious mind. This causes your mind to think of these goals on a continuous basis without you even knowing that it is happening.

I would urge you to think about the most successful person you know, one who has risen to great heights in his or her profession or vocation. You will probably find that this person is driven and exceptionally committed; you might even say that he or she "eats, sleeps, and breathes_____!" Many would probably go as far as saying that they epitomize "greatness" in just about everything they do. This is exactly the type of commitment, energy, and relentless drive for excellence that is associated with mentally tough men and women.

You'll learn more about goal-setting in a subsequent chapter. For now, think about some goals you can set that would require you to extend yourself into a higher level of mental toughness in order to successfully achieve them. Obviously, these goals must be difficult, perhaps even intimidating, if they are to be the vehicle that causes you to stretch beyond you current level of mental toughness.

Think Big!

Set audacious goals!

4. Wake Up Early

In my opinion, this habit—being an early riser—is one that can yield benefits too numerous to list. I also want to state early on that, of the many high-achievers that I personally know (in the military, the business world, academia, etc.), all of them have established the habit of waking up early in the morning–most rising within the 4:30am – 6:00am time window.

What these people have discovered is that by waking up early and taking actions such as working out, meditating, praying, reading, studying, planning, preparing, or a combination of two or more of these actions, over time the cumulative effect of an extra hour or two of dedicated daily effort yields significant results. Many of these people ultimately credit this habit and the extra time it provides each day for much of the success they achieve in their personal and professional lives.

One former special operator who is now a highly-successful entrepreneur told me that getting up earlier and attacking his task list while almost everyone else (including his competition) is still sleeping is his "secret weapon." He, like many other early-risers, feels that he often accomplishes more before 8am than he does during the rest of the day.

I realize that some people reading this will recoil at the thought of getting up an hour or two earlier than usual. Many will declare that "I'm not a morning person" or offer various other reasons why this particular habit won't work for them. To these people, I respectfully say, "Stop making excuses and try it for a week." The human body is very adaptable and within a very short period of time anyone can literally make themselves into a person that not only is able to wake up early each day, but thrives on doing so!

Initially, for some, establishing the habit of waking up early will require them to demonstrate mental toughness because of the mental and physical discomfort they associate with changing their sleep habits. This is actually a good thing as it presents these people with a daily challenge that they can choose to conquer or surrender to. Those who conquer this challenge will have the satisfaction of beginning each day with a small victory (waking up early) that can make possible additional small victories before the sun starts peeking over the horizon. The result of this practice is productive days full of one small victory after another.

5. Try Something New

This step could also be appropriately labeled "Get Outside Your Comfort Zone," and that is precisely what you're going to have to do in order to develop or enhance your mental toughness. Simply stated, you cannot develop mental toughness unless you attempt things that challenge you in a significant way.

This concept is standard among all selection and training courses of special operators. The leaders of SOF units ensure that candidates are continuously exposed to new tasks, procedures, and techniques throughout selection courses. Various "aggravating factors," such as sleep deprivation, hunger, weather (hot and/or cold training environments), increasingly difficult time standards, or other "Go/No-Go" criteria are thrown into the mix to keep candidates off-balance, and in some cases, mentally disoriented while they attempt any number of graded evolutions or tests.

Over time, SOF candidates learn that being required to quickly learn a new skill or perform a certain task to standard (or get dismissed from the selection course!) is not that difficult if they maintain their resolve and focus on "eating the elephant one bite at a time." I can say without reservation that almost all of the special operators I have had the pleasure of working with demonstrated a great amount of eagerness to try and learn new things in their professional and personal lives. These men learned over time that human beings rarely remain at constant levels of mental and physical capacity; they are either getting better or getting worse, but they rarely, if ever, remain at the same level of capability without being challenged on a frequent basis.

The lesson here is that you should continuously strive to push yourself to learn new things and attempt difficult or uncomfortable challenges such as learning a new language, adopting an entirely different workout routine (changing workout partners or perhaps even going to a new gym!) adopting a new hobby, going to new places and meeting new people, etc. Now, doing these things usually brings a measure of discomfort and perhaps even a bit of anxiety to some people. By pushing through the initial thoughts of, "I can't do this" or "Maybe I'll wait until next week," you will take another step toward the next level of mental toughness and the traits and qualities associated with it.

Be bold!

Step outside your comfort zone!

6. Learn How To Control Fear and Stress

To operate effectively in combat situations, special operators must be able to remain focused on the assigned mission, often being required to make rapid decisions while simultaneously performing physical tasks that require both fine and gross motor skills. This is made more difficult by the fact that they are often being shot at or otherwise targeted by a determined enemy force. Success in such situations depends on a mind that is conditioned to expect to feel fear and stress, and knows how to neutralize its impact on human performance in the most stressful conditions imaginable.

Untrained individuals often believe that raw courage is all that is necessary to defeat fear and its effects, and many special operators were once included in this group. As a result of extensive and fairly recent research on this topic, SOF leaders now know that it is critical that every special operator understand the physical and emotional causes of fear, and be able to identify situations in which the body will begin reacting to it.

If one is able to recognize situations that will initiate the body's coping mechanism for fear and stress (the physiological and psychological responses listed in a subsequent chapter) and anticipate their effects on performance, then the proper steps can be taken to thwart these bodily reactions and maintain lower heart rates and, in turn, the ability to perform assigned tasks.

Although impossible to eradicate completely, fear and stress can be effectively controlled to maximize performance during the most challenging situations. Obviously, this capability is something that would be of great benefit to anyone aspiring to develop or enhance their own level of mental toughness.

7. Find a Mentor

Throughout life you've probably had influential people in whom you trust wholeheartedly and respect greatly. Some of these people may be relatives or friends you grew up with. Depending on the situation, some of these people can become a mentor to you.

A mentor is normally someone who has succeeded in accomplishing some of the goals you are striving toward. They are the people you've watched as they work steadily and unwaveringly to attain desired outcomes—be it at work, on a sports team, or during a medical hardship.

A mentor is someone who has taken an interest in you and your goals, and will gladly pass on his or her knowledge on how to attain them. As a mentorship develops and strengthens, you will eventually be able to approach a mentor on significant personal decisions that you need to take in life.

8. Be a Life-Long Learner

Most special operators, in their constant quest for excellence, make it a point to continually feed their hunger for knowledge. As you pursue mental toughness, one of the qualities that you must incorporate to your endeavors is to constantly seek to learn new skills or sharpen existing ones. Find something that interests you, and even if you don't know much about it, take the time to read as much about it as possible. There are many online courses or tutorials on just about any topic you can think of and I encourage you to take advantage of them.

If you pay attention to those who excel in their field, you will find that most of them usually have knowledge of the latest methodology, technique, or trend out there. Most highly efficient people make time to read or study their field, always coming up with innovative ways in which things can be done. Successful special operators are lifelong learners. There have been many instances in which, despite the demanding tempo of their unit, they have found a way to dedicate their own personal time to learn a new skill to employ in real-world situations.

If there is something that you've often thought you might want to learn, find out if there are any courses being offered at your local community college or online university. There are many options open to you in today's world of technology and interconnectedness. You really have no excuse for not finding a way to increase your base of knowledge. Remember knowledge is power, and in difficult situations, having an edge can help you overcome many obstacles.

9. Join Groups of Like-Minded People

When you put a group of like-minded individuals together, you will invariably find that ideas flow, comradery develops, and limits are surpassed. Whatever goal you are seeking to reach, make sure you surround yourself with others who are on that same path. The knowledge you can gain from simple conversations with others who share your same goals is priceless. You will also find the support you need when obstacles arise or the road to your objective becomes difficult.

You probably already realized, before reading this book, that mental toughness is a quality that plays a critical role in achieving high levels of success in all aspects of a person's personal and professional life. While this trait is directly associated with physical toughness in the environments typically associated with special operations units, it is quite often a key ingredient to success in professions and situations in which little or no physical activity takes place.

Regardless of the type of environment you are living or working in, you should be encouraged by knowing that mental toughness can, in fact, be studied and practiced; and individuals from all walks of life can develop this quality to the point where it makes a positive impact on their lives and the attainment of success, however they define it!

Master Sergeant Donald Hollenbaugh and Staff Sergeant Daniel Briggs
U.S. Army – Delta Force

On April 26, 2004, Delta Force operators Master Sergeant Donald Hollenbaugh, Staff Sergeant Daniel Briggs, and a few other special operators joined a platoon of U.S. Marines on a mission to retake the city of Fallujah. As they progressed toward the city, they occupied a position approximately 300 yards forward of American frontlines. As the day dawned the first assault on their position began with a rocket propelled grenade shot by the enemy. The enemy assault resumed with sporadic small arms fire meant for assessing the size of the U.S. forces. Eventually, the attack became more intense and several Marines were wounded in the building adjacent to where Master Sergeant Hollenbaugh was. With a significant number of enemy fighters approaching the two buildings, the situation grew dire.

Staff Sergeant Briggs went out and ran across the road, repeatedly exposing himself to enemy fire, to provide medical care for the wounded in the other building. He located and treated other Marines situated inside the building and also helped evacuate the wounded, all under enemy heavy enemy fire.

Master Sergeant Hollenbaugh and three other men were up on the roof providing defensive fire and tossing grenades along the base of the building in an effort to hold off the encroaching enemy combatants.

As they continued to fight off the attackers and receiving heavy fire in return, a grenade detonated near them and all three of the men fighting alongside of Master Sergeant Hollenbaugh were injured. He moved the wounded Marines to the protection of a nearby stairwell and continued shooting. In order to give the impression that there were more men defending the building than there actually were, Master Sergeant Hollenbaugh alternated shooting from the positions previously held by the wounded.

For approximately an hour Master Sergeant Hollenbaugh maintained his position and continued to provide cover for the evacuation vehicles and for the Marines' to move out of the buildings. After everyone was evacuated, the Marine platoon leader told Hollenbaugh that it was time to go. Both men raced down the stairs and out of the empty house. Hollenbaugh said they linked up with the rest of the platoon a few houses away. It was at that point he realized he had been the only one still defending the house.

For their heroic actions, Master Sergeant Hollenbaugh and Staff Sergeant Briggs were awarded the Distinguished Service Cross.

Master Sergeant Donald Hollenbaugh
CITATION:

For extraordinary heroism in action on 26 April 2004, during combat operations against an armed Iraqi insurgent force while supporting United States Marine Corps operations in Fallujah, Iraq.

Master Sergeant Hollenbaugh demonstrated the highest degree of courage and excellent leadership through his distinguished performance as Team Leader while engaged in Urban Combat Operations. His heroic actions throughout one of the most intensive firefights of the Operation Iraqi Freedom campaign were directly responsible for preventing enemy insurgent forces from overrunning the United States Force. Master Sergeant Hollenbaugh personally eliminated multiple enemy-controlled weapon positions, essential in turning the tide of the enemy's ground-force assault upon a United States Marine Corps Platoon. His actions under fire as a Leader were performed with marked distinction and bravery. Master Sergeant Hollenbaugh's distinctive accomplishments are in keeping with the finest traditions of military service and reflect great credit upon himself, this Command, and the United States Army.

Staff Sergeant Daniel Briggs

CITATION:

For extraordinary heroism in action on 26 April 2004, during combat operations against an armed Iraqi Insurgent force while supporting United States Marine Corps operations in Fallujah, Iraq. Staff Sergeant Briggs repeatedly subjected himself to intense and unrelenting enemy fire in order to provide critical medical attention to severely injured Marines and organized defensive operations. He set the highest example of personal bravery through his demonstrated valor and calmness under fire. Staff Sergeant Briggs' valiant actions prevented enemy insurgent forces from over-running the United States Force's position and were directly responsible for prevention of additional United States military casualties or Prisoners of War by the enemy. His actions under fire as a combat medic were performed with marked distinction and bravery. Staff Sergeant Briggs' distinctive accomplishments are in keeping with the finest traditions of the military service and reflect great credit upon himself, this command, and the United States Army.

The Wet Socks Story

Any veteran of a SOF unit will tell you that it is not always the most physically qualified candidates who pass selection; in fact, it is often quite the opposite. Once physically exhausted or mentally fatigued from nearly continuous training events, tests, and assessments, many perfectly-qualified candidates simply lose the resolve they once had and decide to quit the selection course.

Countless studies have been conducted by SOF units in an attempt to identify critical traits and capabilities required to pass selection and enable a man to go on to perform well in a SOF unit. Despite their efforts, however, no SOF unit has been able to come up with an infallible formula that will render guaranteed results for every single candidate. The reason for this is that those qualities that often enable a candidate to succeed against the odds are unquantifiable and intangible.

The same is true of most environments. If you think about it, you have probably met individuals who, despite having the "ideal" education, training, and background for a job or role, simply fail miserably. Likewise, you probably have met individuals who lack all the advantages and have to fight tooth and nail every step of the way, and yet they are the ones who persevere and excel.

I had a conversation with a 30-year SOF veteran who once held a key role in the selection course for his unit. He told me that seeing so many highly-qualified men quit the course made him realize that there was no real way of predicting who would make it and who would not. He told me that when prospective candidates would tell him about their experiences running triathlons, marathons, martial arts, etc., he would politely say to them: "That's very impressive. We'll have to find out if you can do it when your socks are wet."

The candidates would often be confused by his statement because they didn't yet comprehend what he was really saying: that a man's prior experiences, achievements, and levels of physical strength and endurance under normal circumstances did not necessarily mean that he could perform as well once he was exhausted, hungry, dehydrated, and while dealing with nagging injuries and exceptionally high levels of mental, emotional, and physical stress.

This highly-experienced special operator first heard the "wet socks" concept from a senior sergeant in the training and operations section of a foreign counter-terrorist unit where he was assigned for an exchange tour. He had had to pass the selection course for this unit in order to remain in this assignment, and after doing so, he was then fully integrated into an operational squadron for three years. During the course of many conversations with the host-nation's sergeant, the topic of selection and why some men pass and some don't was often discussed.

During one of these conversations, the sergeant reminded him of an event during selection in which the group of candidates had to traverse a long distance, over very hilly terrain, while carrying heavy rucksacks. This event was quite difficult because each man had to complete it within an undisclosed time frame or be removed from the course.

The sergeant asked him, "Do you remember running the same event about 10 days later? But that time the entire class was ordered to run into a nearby stream and get themselves entirely soaked from head to toe?" He then went on to say, "Over the years we noticed that the top finishers in the "dry run" were almost never the same as those of the "wet run." More importantly, we realized that more of the top finishers of the "wet run" successfully completed selection than did their "dry run" counterparts."

The lesson as explained by the sergeant, was that it became obvious that some men were capable of performing quite well under ideal or normal conditions, but were thrown off-balance or otherwise negatively affected by the sudden introduction of unexpected factors or conditions. Having to run the event with soaking wet clothing, boots, and socks meant that the men would almost certainly have problems with them slipping off their feet, bunching up and causing great discomfort and usually painful blisters on their feet.

Anyone who has ever had to conduct a military-style forced march while carrying a heavy rucksack, wearing body armor and carrying a weapon, will truly understand how much stress and physical discomfort can arise from something as seemingly irrelevant as one's sock being wet. Add to that the pressure and stresses associated with a SOF selection course and you can understand how it will cause a man to have to tap into his reservoir of mental toughness and drive on with unwavering motivation and resolve.

The moral of the "wet socks story" is that, ultimately, all that matters is your ability to perform well at the critical moment, regardless of environmental conditions or unexpected circumstances. Whether you are an athlete or not, you probably know of some individuals, teammates, or competitors who perform brilliantly in practice or less important events, yet always seem to perform badly when the stakes are the highest.

As you set your sights on your goals or dreams and start on the path to achieving them, you probably already know that there will be times and situations that will force you to "dig deep." You must figure out a way to stay focused and motivated as you follow your plan; and like the men going through the selection course mentioned earlier, it is highly likely that you'll have to do this while pushing through whatever form of "wet socks" situations arise during your journey. Personal and professional stress, uncertainty, fatigue, injury, anxiety, and self-doubt are just a few examples of things that can potentially distract you or otherwise cause you to lose focus.

You will require a great amount of determination and resilience in order to surmount the obstacles that will invariably stand in your way. Fortunately, as you will discover in subsequent chapters, there are traits and skills that you can develop in order to overcome difficult, stressful situations, and enable you to enhance your mental toughness—that intangible characteristic that often determines whether you attain your goals, or just give up.

Gunnery Sergeant Brian Jacklin
U.S. Marine Corps Special Operations Command

On June 14, 2012, while performing village stability operations in the Upper Gereshk Valley of Afghanistan's Helmand Province, a Marine Corps special operations team found themselves surrounded on the rooftop of a village compound. Under heavy enemy gunfire, their team leader and another team member were critically wounded. At that point Gunnery Sergeant Brian Jacklin took charge of the situation, managing to establish alternate communications in order to direct fire support from a nearby unit as well as coordinate medical evacuation for his wounded team members.

With the medical evacuation helicopter on its way, Gunnery Sergeant Jacklin led his team out of the compound in order to establish a landing zone for the evacuation. They had to traverse through open terrain while still under heavy fire. Gunnery Sergeant Jacklin and his team were able to provide suppressing fire with an M203 grenade launcher until the casualties were able to be evacuated and flown to safety

Despite being reinforced by another special operations unit, Gunnery Sergeant Jacklin decided to remain behind and continue to fight. Throughout that whole day, and during an intense battle fought the next day, he exemplified resilience, determination, and courage. He was a true inspiration for all who fought alongside him to defeat the enemy force.

On April 9, 2015, Gunnery Sergeant Brian Jacklin was awarded the Navy Cross for his extraordinary valor.

CITATION:

For extraordinary heroism while serving with the 1st Marine Special Operations Battalion in support of Operation ENDURING FREEDOM. On the morning of 14 June 2012 Gunnery Sergeant Jacklin was second in command of a team conducting village stability operations in the volatile Upper Gereshk Valley of Helmand Province. The enemy suddenly poured heavy fire into the team's position, and his team leader and another Marine each suffered life threatening gunshot wounds. Without hesitation, Gunnery Sergeant Jacklin seized control of the situation and orchestrated a counterattack. Finding the primary communications link inoperable, he personally established an alternate means with a nearby supporting unit and began prosecuting direct, indirect, and aviation fires on the enemy, while simultaneously coordinating evacuation of the casualties. He courageously led his team out of their compound and through open terrain in order to secure a landing zone, but enemy ground fire initially forced the casevac aircraft to wave off. Gunnery Sergeant Jacklin voluntarily remained behind, and throughout a raging battle all the next day, he provided vital intelligence, tactical assistance, and deadly accurate personal fires. Throughout 48 hours, he inspired all around him as he led a vicious fight to defeat a determined enemy force. By his decisive actions, bold initiative, and complete dedication to duty, Gunnery Sergeant Jacklin reflected great credit upon himself and the Marine Corps and upheld the highest traditions of the United States Naval Service.

Fear and Stress

To learn how to control fear and stress, you must first understand your body's natural response to these conditions. Fear stimulates the sympathetic nervous system, which is responsible for the fight-or-flight response that is programmed into our brains as a result of millions of years of human evolution. This response has been present since the first cavemen fought with one another over food and faced off against wild predators.

Fear elicits a stimulation of the sympathetic nervous system while a human is under stress, called "threat stress." This stimulation or "arousal" triggers a hormonal response—release of adrenaline and cortisol—within the human nervous system; it is a built-in coping and survival mechanism that all humans possess. If a combat soldier isn't properly trained to control the effects of this hormonal reaction, his performance and level of execution will be greatly diminished. The same is true of any person who faces a dangerous or threatening situation and isn't trained to control this response

Physiological Responses: Once a threat is perceived, the immediate response of the body is the sudden release of adrenaline, norepinephrine, and cortisol. This hormonal release causes certain reactions in the human body:

- An increase in heart and respiratory rate.
- The blood vessels of your muscles are dilated in order to increase the transport of oxygen resulting in an increase of power and energy. Conversely, the blood vessels to other organs are constricted in order to avoid blood loss in case of injury.
- Glucose is released into the bloodstream to aid in increase of energy to the musculatory system.
- You experience dryness of the mouth due to salivation glands becoming inhibited.
- Pupils dilate in order to enhance vision.
- The muscles controlling your bladder and bowels become relaxed.
- Decreased peripheral vision.
- Loss of control of reflexes, sometimes resulting in uncontrolled shaking.
- Increased sweating.

Psychological Responses: Due to the severity of some of the physical reactions the human body undergoes while under stress, there are some psychological responses that occur as a consequence. Normal mental processes become compromised and a state of panic may occur rendering you incapable of simple cognitive tasks. The following are some of the effects that result from severe stress:

- Loss of concentration and effectiveness. Paralysis—inability to act—may occur.

- Inability to focus on anything other than the threat—tunnel vision—will result in an inability to consider the situation as a whole and act accordingly in order to defeat or deter the immediate danger.

- The brain can become incapable of processing ancillary sensory information such as hearing.

- When facing danger or threat, the mind might store information differently than how events actually occur. The time sequence might differ, or the actual events might differ from how they were perceived during the stress of a dangerous situation.

The Response Cycle: Dr. Roger Solomon is a highly regarded psychologist and psychotherapist specializing in the areas of trauma and grief. He proposes that there are stages that take place when you are facing a life threatening or otherwise highly stressful situation. The faster a person can recognize and progress through these stages, the greater the chance of overcoming the situation he or she is facing. Here are the five stages of the response cycle:

1. **Alarm.** The initial realization that danger is imminent.

2. **Capability Assessment.** The assessment of your ability to cope with the situation. This stage can either propel you into action or paralyze you.

3. **Redirection of Focus.** If you have been trained to handle fear and stress, this is the stage during which you will be able to redirect your thoughts and focus toward a plan of action. Practice and rehearsal are a vital part of being able to execute during this stage.

4. **Skill Reactivation.** Once you have successfully redirected your focus, your instincts will kick in and the skills you have practiced endlessly will be activated and become more automatic.

5. **Action.** You make a decision to commit to a plan of action and go for it.

The key to being able to respond effectively to a threat and ensure survival is to gain an understanding of what is happening in your body, anticipating the normal responses your body will undergo, and learning how to regain control.

How to Control Fear and Stress

The ability to recognize the psychological and physiological effects fear has on the human body is the first step in learning to control fear. In order to learn how to overcome these effects and be able to effectively carry out a mission or task requires practice.

It was once widely believed that raw courage was all that was necessary in order to overcome fear. Special operators now know that knowledge and understanding of the symptoms produced by fear is critical. Just as the body responds to the physiological responses of the brain, there are proven methods for countering the responses that will help neutralize them and allow you to function effectively and successfully carry out your mission.

It is important to understand that experiencing fear does not signify cowardice. In fact, it is the ability to remain calm and continue to perform—despite the fear—that shows true courage. Studies have shown that it is the belief of eight out of ten combat veterans, that you are better off admitting that you are afraid, discussing your fears, and deciding a plan of action before you enter into battle.

Discussing fear has never been easy for special operators, and probably never will be. Because they are almost all driven, Type-A personalities used to overcoming significant obstacles and performing much better than most "normal" men, these warriors are often reluctant to admit that they have any weaknesses, even those that they were born with. But the leaders within SOF units recognized that utilizing the information gained from various studies on this topic could enable them to enhance the performance of their operators as well as to help otherwise capable candidates successfully complete selection courses.

How Navy SEALs Control Fear and Stress

Through the evolution of Special Operations in the United States, new research and knowledge has been developed, which has led to the adoption of various methods and techniques for adequately handling fear and stress. Although some of these are classified and cannot be shared with the public, the Naval Special Warfare community has freely shared extensive amounts of information regarding how Navy SEALs are trained to address their reactions to the human stress response. This information can be of great value to you as you prepare your body and mind for the challenge you are planning to accept. As you read on, think about how you might integrate some of this knowledge into your personal training program.

Today, all prospective Navy SEALs are taught the *Seven Pillar Technique* and the *Rapid Response Technique* (Note: these techniques are often referred to by a variety of different names and descriptors) as a way of maintaining their resolve and motivation in the face of stress and fear. Likewise, SEALs in operational units now understand that the body's reactions to situations associated with threat stress are as normal and predictable as when one is holding his breath while swimming underwater or when the body is subjected to prolonged cold that leads to hypothermia.

SEALs (and members of other SOF units) now understand that what used to be attributed solely to "guts" is actually a man's ability to use his mind to anticipate and identify any situation that will trigger one or more of the body's physical responses to fear. Countering these responses early on will enable them to remain calm and effective on the battlefield.

The Navy SEAL Seven Pillars of Mental Toughness

1. Goal Setting and Segmenting

Studies conducted by Navy psychologists revealed that some of the BUD/S candidates who failed to make it through training admitted that they allowed themselves to become overwhelmed by the fact that there was still a considerable amount of training still remaining in the course.

Some of these candidates became besieged by the knowledge that the vast majority of men did not typically graduate from the course, and that the training events and tests ahead of them would only become more and more difficult as the course progressed. Their negative thoughts resulted in poor performance that led to their dismissal from the course, or they simply quit and gave up on their dream.

In contrast, the researchers showed that almost all the candidates who had successfully completed the course and then went on to serve as SEALs, had used a technique in which they established short-term, mid-term, and long-term goals for themselves throughout BUD/S and the many months of follow-on training. This technique is referred to as "segmenting" or "chunking." It essentially breaks down larger goals into smaller and more manageable pieces or phases.

Segmenting the course meant that, instead of dwelling on the fact that they were facing many weeks of training ahead of them, most successful trainees would instead focus on that specific training day and further segment the day into several stages. Candidates following this method would first focus on making it through the early morning physical training session. During this session, they'd think of nothing but the specific exercise they were doing at the time. Then, their complete focus would go to the next exercise dictated by the instructor leading the session, and then the next one after that and so forth until the session ended.

Once physical training was over, the next segment of the day would be to get cleaned up and make sure their barracks rooms were ready for inspection. Once the room inspection was completed, the class would run to a classroom for several periods of instruction.

During this period of several hours, the trainees would focus only on the class being taught. After the classes were completed, the trainees would be directed to the obstacle course for a "timed run," which many trainees found quite challenging and stressful due to the rather severe consequences if they failed to meet the time requirements. Because of the serious consequences, some of the BUD/S trainees allow themselves to dwell on this event during earlier portions of the day, and as a result lose focus during the preceding training evolutions, which could cause them to fail an evaluation or otherwise incur the wrath of the instructors. In some instances they would become so anxious and nervous about the timed run of the obstacle course, that their energy and concentration would be greatly diminished by the time they actually ran the course. The consequence of this energy-draining worry was poor performance during the graded evolution.

By focusing solely on each segment of the day at a time, successful BUD/S trainees avoided focusing on the rather dreadful fact that they had many long months of exceptionally difficult training ahead. They segmented the grueling six-month course into months, weeks, days, and then each day into several *"chunks"* of time and they focused on successfully completing them one at a time.

Goal setting and segmentation are time-tested techniques that you should consider utilizing as you strive to achieve excellence.

2. Arousal Control

As discussed previously, when a person is exposed to stressful situations that trigger the human stress response, his or her brain will automatically initiate a chemical reaction that will produce almost immediate effects on certain bodily functions and a range of emotions. This arousal response is a perfectly normal and predictable reaction by human beings, but it can also have a negative impact on a person's critical thinking, decision making, and fine motor skills.

For special operators, allowing themselves to become negatively affected by emotions such as anger, fear or anxiety is not conducive to combat effectiveness. One of the methods used by special operators is a controlled breathing technique called the 4x4 breathing. It consists of slowly breathing in to the count of 4 and then exhaling slowly through the mouth, again to the count of 4. If you repeat this cycle for at least four minutes, you'll find that your heart rate will slow down and any nervousness or anxiety that you may be experiencing will begin to lessen. I recommend that you experiment with this breathing technique and see how it works for you.

3. Visualization

Visualization is a technique that has been used by high-level athletes for many years, and, to varying degrees, most SOF units have gradually adopted and increased its use over the past decade or so.

The way this technique works is to visualize a scenario that may occur during a combat operation. The special operator tries to predict how they will react to various elements; what tactics or actions they will need to employ given certain changes or unforeseen events. Not only do they visualize what they see, but also what they might feel, hear, or even smell.

Through repetition of this exercise, the operator will be able to develop a plan of action for the various scenarios that may present themselves. In this way, when an operator actually faces the situation, though it may be the first time he is physically engaged in it, in his mind he has already gone over it numerous times. This state of readiness in his mind serves to preempt the stress responses that would arise otherwise.

For example, during BUD/S training, students wearing SCUBA gear and submerged under water, are required to correctly execute various emergency procedures and corrective actions to resolve problems with their equipment. The evolution consist of instructors will conducting an attack on the students and snatching the regulators from their mouths, closing the SCUBA-tank air valves, disconnecting hoses from the tanks, or tying the hoses in knots. Most of the students are still very new to being underwater and wearing SCUBA gear; and they are not yet completely comfortable and confident in this environment.

The stress that ensues from such an attack, could lead a student to panic and surface before completing the exercise. Rushing through the motions of the exercise or failing to meet the established time parameters will also result in failure. Failure to pass after a few attempts will require the candidate to be recycled to another BUD/S class, or depending on other factors, removal from the program altogether.

Studies by Navy psychologists found that most of the men who had successfully passed this exercise on the first attempt used some form of visualization prior to the event. Despite feeling the same degree of anxiety and apprehension as their peers, they had repeatedly visualized the actions they needed to execute through the emergency situations. As a result of this visualization, once the evolution was actually underway, the students were able to effectively ignore or cope with the fact that they were being attacked and focused entirely on calmly solving the problems being presented to them.

Visualization and mental-rehearsal techniques have been used for many years by people in various professions and sports that are associated with high-risk/high-stress situations. Chances are that you have already engaged in some degree of visualization if you have participated in sports. Using this technique not only provides your mind the opportunity to engage in a series of rehearsals, it also sharpens your focus and helps you avoid distractions when you are working toward reaching a specific goal. I urge you to adopt and incorporate this technique into your daily life and practice it as much as possible!

4. Positive Self-Talk

The knowledge of the importance of positive self-talk has long been of interest to psychologists. It is widely known that it can have a positive impact on a person as they undergo periods of great stress or anxiety; or when they are engaged in the pursuit of a significant and highly desired personal or professional goal, objective, prize, achievement, or form of recognition. For individuals attempting to develop a strong, confident, and resilient mindset, positive self-talk is a critical technique to engage in.

Research studies have shown that the average person thinks at a rate of 1,000 to 5,000 words per minute. Even when a person is alone, sitting silently, there is an active "conversation" taking place within his or her mind. The quality of these conversations is totally within our control. It is the individual's choice whether to constantly berate him or herself, or to constantly build up self-confidence through positive reinforcement.

Reflect upon the "conversations" you've had with yourself prior to some difficult task or challenge and you will probably realize that your performance was directly affected, positively or negatively, by your state of mind and what you were thinking.

Throughout SOF selection courses, the young candidates are constantly faced with tests and graded evolutions of ever-increasing difficulty. A student in any of these courses will often 'talk to himself' hundreds of times per day. The determination to achieve their goal to serve in a SOF unit is a constant topic for the self-talk in which these young men engage. They focus on achieving their objective and convince themselves that nothing, no amount of pain will cause them to fail to achieve their goal. The use of positive self-talk continues after successfully completing a selection course and throughout subsequent service in a SOF unit.

You'd be wise to adopt and refine the use of the self-talk technique. It is perhaps the single most valuable tool that you can use to develop the mindset, confidence, and resilience needed to achieve your goals.

5. Compartmentalization

The grim reality of warfare means that special operators will inevitably experience various types of emotions. These men are taught to expect casualties within their units once actual combat begins and seeing comrades, some of whom are close personal friends, seriously wounded or killed can produce various reactions such as sadness, anger, and, of course, fear.

The mission must come first, and emotions have to take a back seat until the time is right. During combat operations, special operators must temporarily suspend their natural reactions to fear and the death and destruction that may be going on around them. They learn to suppress normal human responses to extreme stress during the actual fight, knowing that they'll be able to address their emotions, the loss of friends, and other trauma at a later time, when it is safe to do so.

Fortunately it is unlikely that you will witness or experience something this traumatic during your personal or professional life. However, the sooner you adopt this technique of compartmentalization the better. For instance, if you experience a setback at school, at work or in some other aspect of your personal life, you must be able to *"shake it off"* and remain focused on your goals.

6. Contingency Planning

Another technique used to minimize an individual's response to fear or stress is contingency planning. This technique is closely aligned with visualization. In preparation for upcoming missions, special operators will, if they have enough time to do so, dissect the entire operation from start to finish. They will discuss what the plan is, as well as all alternate actions that will be taken if, for various reasons, the plan becomes untenable and rapid adjustments need to be made in order to achieve success.

All special operators know that the likelihood of battle plans going off without a hitch is rare. Admitting this prior to execution in combat has a very specific advantage. This awareness will allow them to individually and collectively prepare for what may happen at various stages of the operation, and prepare a viable plan of action. This enables units and individual operators to adjust the battle plan, with little or no hesitation, during critical phases of an operation when lives are at stake and momentum must be maintained.

Thinking about what can happen during an event, and knowing that you have already thought about what actions you will take is a very powerful confidence builder. This confidence also enables rapid reaction to an obstacle or setback, which in turn enables you to avoid your body's normal response to stressors. Simply put, it's not about what happens during an important event or graded evolution, it's what you do in response to what happens that counts. Engaging in contingency planning is a superb way to enhance your chances of success in all aspects of your life!

7. Focus and Concentration

Because of the dangerous nature and the high-stress/high risk environments in which special operations take place, a great amount of focus and concentration from each individual involved is required. Operators must therefore train and work very hard to sharpen their concentration and ability to focus during exercises and real-world operations.

Distractions of various types are the main impediment to proper focus and concentration. Over time, you can develop specific and tailored routines to help you avoid being distracted during situations where the need for intense focus and concentration is high.

Unplanned Events

The "fog of war" is the chaos that occurs during battles in combat. Regardless of how well developed a battle plan may be, it is inevitable that there will be unforeseen events that can derail it. To deal with the setback and deviations of a plan, special operators revert to a modified version of The Seven Pillar Technique known as the Rapid Response Technique.

Rapid Response Technique

1. Arousal control.
2. Self-Talk.
3. Assess the situation relative to any threat to:
   a. Your personal safety and survival, and that of your teammates
   b. Accomplishing the mission
4. Consider appropriate courses of action and responses.
5. Take action.
6. Assess.
7. Repeat this cycle until the mission is accomplished or the situation is resolved.

SEALs are constantly exposed to training that replicates the tempo, stress, and physical and mental demands of actual combat situations, which provides them with almost unlimited opportunities to utilize these techniques to control their body's response to fear and threat stress. Although you may not be presented with life-threatening situations in your daily life, you can still adopt these techniques when faced with stressful or difficult situations.

Use These Techniques!

As mentioned previously, knowledge and understanding of the physical responses to fear is the first step in learning how to control your reactions. The methods mentioned in this chapter will allow you to remain calm and in control during stressful situations. You should experiment with the seven techniques discussed in this chapter and utilize them in a manner that best enhances your ability to cope with fear, stress, anxiety, and any other physical and mental responses you may experience as you pursue your goals.

Technical Sergeant John Chapman
U.S. Air Force Combat Controller

On March 4, 2002, Technical Sergeant John Chapman, an Air Force Combat Controller, was involved in a reconnaissance mission in northern Afghanistan when his team's twin-engine Chinook helicopter came under heavy fire, was hit by a rocket-propelled grenade and crash-landed on the top of a mountain.

Technical Sergeant Chapman called in air support to cover the team, which was now exposed to a high-volume of enemy fire. He also directed a helicopter rescue of his team and aircrew members and led the search for a Navy SEAL who had fallen from the helicopter. Technical Sergeant Chapman killed two enemy fighters during the search, but came upon a machine-gun nest. Though the enemy fired on the rescue team on three sides, Chapman continued to fight. Soon, however, multiple wounds claimed his life, though he is credited with saving the lives of the others in the rescue team and enabling them to continue to battle the enemy.

On January 10, 2003, Technical Sergeant John Chapman was posthumously awarded the Air Force Cross for his extraordinary valor.

CITATION:

For extraordinary heroism in military operation against an armed enemy of the United States as a 24th Special Tactics Squadron, Combat

Controller in the vicinity of Gardez, in the eastern highlands of Afghanistan, on 4 March 2002. On this date, during his helicopter insertion for a reconnaissance and time sensitive targeting close air support mission, Sergeant Chapman's aircraft came under heavy machine gun fire and received a direct hit from a rocket propelled grenade which caused a United States Navy sea-air-land team member to fall from the aircraft. Though heavily damaged, the aircraft egressed the area and made an emergency landing seven kilometers away. Once on the ground Sergeant Chapman established communication with an AC-130 gunship to insure the area was secure while providing close air support coverage for the entire team. He then directed the gunship to begin the search for the missing team member. He requested, coordinated, and controlled the helicopter that extracted the stranded team and aircrew members. These actions limited the exposure of the aircrew and team to hostile fire. Without regard for his own life Sergeant Chapman volunteered to rescue his missing team member from an enemy strong hold. Shortly after insertion, the team made contact with the enemy. Sergeant Chapman engaged and killed two enemy personnel. He continued to advance reaching the enemy position then engaged a second enemy position, a dug-in machine gun nest. At this time the rescue team came under effective enemy fire from three directions. From close range he exchanged fire with the enemy from minimum personal cover until he succumbed to multiple wounds. His engagement and destruction of the first enemy position and advancement on the second position enabled his team to move to cover and break enemy contact. In his own words, his

Navy sea-air-land team leader credits Sergeant Chapman unequivocally with saving the lives of the entire rescue team. Through his extraordinary heroism, superb airmanship, aggressiveness in the face of the enemy, and the dedication to the service of his country, Sergeant Chapman reflects the highest credit upon himself and the United States Air Force.

Confidence

According to the Merriam-Webster's Collegiate Dictionary, confidence can be defined as follows:

1. "a feeling or consciousness of one's powers or of reliance on one's circumstances,"

2. "faith or belief that one will act in a right, proper, or effective way," and

3. "the quality or state of being certain."

Self-confidence is a quality that lies at the very heart of this book, and is definitely one that you will want to strive to increase as you pursue a goal or objective. For the purposes of this chapter—and throughout the entire book—the terms *confidence* and *self-confidence* will be used interchangeably.

The Importance of Self-Confidence

Self-confidence is an essential quality for anyone to have in any situation, especially when seeking to achieve an objective. It is one of the most critical traits for any candidate attempting to become a special operator, and without it, it is almost impossible to complete any of the SOF selection courses. Confidence is the cornerstone of the mental toughness that members of special operations units are famous for and exhibit on a daily basis during training and combat operations. It has been proven many times over that a high-level of confidence enables special operators to establish high goals and to persevere while achieving them.

In his book *Unbeatable Mind*, author and retired Navy SEAL Mark Divine said:

> *The self-confidence of a SEAL is both a character trait and a skill. The skill is to rack up small, worthy, and achievable victories on the way to mission accomplishment. In addition, it requires being able to reframe failures to find a silver lining. With these two skills, you will have the self-confidence to attack any challenge, and your confidence in your domain of expertise will grow as your success grows.*

In my experience, if there's one trait that Navy SEALs and members of other SOF units embody, it is self-confidence and this, of course, is at the core of how these men develop and maintain a high-level of mental toughness.

Confidence is Contagious

In any arena, whether it's business, academia, the medical field, or sports you will have noticed that confident and successful people tend to associate personally and professionally with others possessing the same qualities. Anyone who is known to be at the highest levels of competence and achievement is typically surrounded by other high-level performers.

Sayings that you may have heard growing up—"Birds of a feather flock together" or "You become who you associate with"— probably have already proven to be true in some way in your life.

These concepts also hold true within the special operations community. The few candidates who possess the necessary traits to make it through selection and then go on to serve in a SOF unit will be surrounded by many other supremely confident and competent peers, seniors, and subordinates. By default, this serves to maintain and enhance, in each individual, the core characteristics that epitomize everything a SOF operator needs to be.

Confidence Is Visible

The way you carry yourself will often be the determining factor on whether you succeed or fail to attain an objective. When you demonstrate control of yourself, your emotions, and the situation, those around you will recognize you as a leader and will be willing to follow you. SOF operators are normally recognizable by an aura of quiet confidence that is undeniable. Their steady, resolute demeanor inspires trust and confidence to anyone around them.

Indicators of Low Self-Confidence

We all know people who are lacking in self-confidence. My personal observations have shown that these people usually share some of the following traits and behavior patterns:

- **Complaining.** Insecure people use complaining as a way of diverting attention from their shortcomings. Those who constantly complain are often insecure people, who are incapable of taking responsibility for themselves or their actions.

- **Showing Off.** Typically, people tend to show off in order to get attention or recognition. If you are sure of yourself and your abilities, then your actions will speak louder than words. Your achievements and triumphs will be the testament to what you are capable of. It is those who lack confidence in themselves, their skills, and their social standing who need to compensate by showing off.

- **Addictions.** Because of a lack of confidence and a feeling of inadequacy, some people might turn to destructive habits or behaviors, such as drug or alcohol abuse.

- **Constant Need for Approval.** A lack of self-confidence can be evidenced by the need of constant praise or approval. This constant craving for praise will become an obstacle that will stand in the way of anyone seeking to reach a high level of achievement. A candidate won't make it through a SOF selection course, nor will he last long in a special operations unit if he needs *any* form of approval from the instructor staff, his peers, or his superiors.

- **Self-Pity.** Regardless how dangerous or stressful a situation may be, the first step to defeat is self-pity. Once you allow any thoughts of quitting to enter your mind, you are giving way to failure. Feeling sorry for yourself in any situation will deplete your self-confidence and guarantee your downfall.

Developing Self-Confidence

Confidence results from a range of experiences and actions that you take over the course of your life. Increasing your level of self-confidence will require some work. Fortunately this is not a task that takes years to achieve. Although it varies depending on each individual's situation, augmenting your level of confidence can be accomplished in a matter of weeks or even days.

Although special operators typically do not lack confidence, their methods and techniques will serve to help those who may need to develop it. There is no standard prescription that can guarantee a person will become more confident, but the following steps will greatly aid in the process:

1. Set a Personal or Professional Goal. If you haven't done so already, you should clearly define what you are trying to accomplish—your goal or objective. Your goal can be something you've already attempted to do in the past, but for whatever reason were unable to attain it, or it can be something you've always wanted to do, but were unsure of how to do it. All you need to do is simply decide that the time has come to finally embark on the journey!

2. Prepare Yourself. Once you've set your goal, the obvious next step is to chart your course. I've always enjoyed this aspect of goal setting, actually doing the research and investigation into what it is going to take to achieve a goal or objective. I find that learning about what is associated with achieving a goal is, in itself, a confidence builder. The content found in the **Preparation and Practice** and the **Setting Goals** chapters will help you formulate a plan of action.

3. Visualize Success. By now you have learned how important it is to actually visualize yourself achieving your goal. The fact that the Navy SEALs have included it as one of the pillars in the Seven Pillar Technique, and members of other SOF units utilize this technique should reinforce just how essential to success visualization is. Achieving whatever it is that you desire to do hinges on your belief and ability to envision yourself succeeding.

I think you'll agree that people lacking confidence are more likely to believe that their success—or lack thereof—depends more on fate or on what others do to them or for them. They seem to have a feeling of hopelessness and resignation that the highest level of success, whatever that means to them personally, is out of reach and unattainable. This is not the mindset or attitude associated with successful people, and it is certainly not how special operators approach life. You have the ability to directly and immediately increase your level of self-confidence—believe it!

Master Sergeant Gordon and Sergeant First Class Randall Shughart
U.S. Army – Delta Force

On October 3, 1993, Delta Force Master Sergeant Gary Gordon was serving as a sniper team leader on a mission in Mogadishu, Somalia. The purpose of the mission was to capture the Somali warlord Mohamed Aidid, or any of his top advisers. Master Sergeant Gordon and Sergeant First Class Randall Shughart were providing sniper cover from a helicopter during the assault.

When the call came in that an American helicopter had been shot down somewhere in the city, a search and rescue team was sent out to provide aid and secure the crash site. Soon though, the news came that another helicopter had also been shot down.

With a large number of Somali forces moving toward the crash site, supporting ground forces were unable to make their way to help the downed crew. Frustrated by their inability to provide much help from the air, the Delta operators requested to be inserted at the second crash site to protect the wounded crew. Due to significant enemy force movement, their request was denied three times before they were allowed to be dropped into the scene.

Armed with only their personal weapons, Gordon and Shughart were dropped near the site to engage the enemy. After fighting their way through heavy enemy fire, they finally arrived at the crash site, where they found the wounded Black Hawk pilot, Mike Durant, as well as the rest of the crew members and removed them from the wreckage. They managed to inflict heavy casualties on the enemy, but with their ammunition nearly exhausted, they were outnumbered and overtaken by the enemy. Despite their valiant efforts to secure the crash site, Gordon and Shughart were killed by enemy fire.

For their extraordinary courage, Master Sergeant Gordon and Sergeant First Class Randall Shughart were both awarded the Medal of Honor, America's highest award for battlefield valor.

Master Sergeant Gary Gordon

CITATION:

For gallantry and intrepidity at the risk of life above and beyond the call of duty, on 3 October 1993, while serving as Sniper Team Leader, United States Army Special Operations Command with Task Force Ranger in Mogadishu, Somalia, in support of Operation RSTORE HOPE. On that date, Master Sergeant Gordon's sniper team provided precision fires from the lead helicopter during an assault and at two helicopter crash sites, while subjected to intense automatic weapons and rocket propelled grenade fires. When Master Sergeant Gordon learned that ground forces were not immediately available to secure the second crash site, he and another sniper unhesitatingly volunteered to be inserted to protect the four critically wounded personnel, despite being well aware of the growing number of enemy personnel closing in on the site. After his third request to be inserted, Master Sergeant Gordon received permission to perform his volunteer mission. When debris and enemy ground fires at the site caused them to abort the first attempt, Master Sergeant Gordon was inserted one hundred meters south of the crash site. Equipped with only his sniper rifle and a pistol, Master Sergeant Gordon and his fellow sniper, while under intense small arms fire from the enemy, fought their way through a dense maze of shanties and shacks to reach the critically injured crew members. Master Sergeant Gordon immediately pulled the pilot and the other crew members from the aircraft, establishing a perimeter which placed him and his fellow sniper in the most vulnerable position. Master Sergeant Gordon used his long range rifle and side arm to kill an undetermined number of attackers until he depleted his ammunition. Master Sergeant Gordon then went back to the wreckage, recovering some of the crew's weapons and ammunition. Despite the fact that he was critically low on ammunition, he provided some of it to the dazed pilot and then radioed for help. Master Sergeant Gordon continued to travel the perimeter, protecting the downed crew. After his team member was fatally wounded and his own rifle ammunition exhausted, Master Sergeant Gordon returned to the wreckage, recovering a rifle with the last five rounds of ammunition and gave it to the pilot with the words, "good luck." Then, armed only with his pistol, Master Sergeant Gordon continued to fight until he was fatally wounded. His actions saved the pilot's life. Master Sergeant Gordon's extraordinary heroism and devotion to duty were in keeping with the highest standards of military service and reflect great credit upon, his unit and the United States Army.

Sergeant First Class Randall Shugart
CITATION:

For gallantry and intrepidity at the risk of life above and beyond the call of duty, on 3 October 1993, while serving as a Sniper Team Member, United States Army Special Operations Command with Task Force Ranger in Mogadishu, Somalia, in support of Operation RESTORE HOPE. On that date, Sergeant First Class Shughart provided precision sniper fires from the lead helicopter during an assault on a building and at two helicopter crash sites, while subjected to intense automatic weapons and rocket propelled grenade fires. While providing critical suppressive fires at the second crash site, Sergeant First Class Shughart and his team leader learned that ground forces were not immediately available to secure the site. Sergeant First Class Shughart and his team leader unhesitatingly volunteered to be inserted to protect the four critically wounded personnel, despite being well aware of the growing number of enemy personnel closing in on the site. After their third request to be inserted, Sergeant First Class Shughart and his team leader received permission to perform this volunteer mission. When debris and enemy ground fires at the site caused them to abort the first attempt, Sergeant First Class Shughart and his team leader were inserted one hundred meters south of the crash site. Equipped with only his sniper rifle and a pistol, Sergeant First Class Shughart and his team leader, while under intense small arms fire from the enemy, fought their way through a dense maze of shanties and shacks to reach the critically injured crew members. Sergeant First Class Shughart pulled the pilot and the other crew members from the aircraft, establishing a perimeter which placed him and his fellow sniper in the most vulnerable position. Sergeant First Class Shughart used his long range rifle and side arm to kill an undetermined number of attackers while traveling the perimeter, protecting the downed crew. Sergeant First Class Shughart continued his protective fire until he depleted his ammunition and was fatally wounded. His actions saved the pilot's life. Sergeant First Class Shughart's extraordinary heroism and devotion to duty were in keeping with the highest standards of military service and reflect great credit upon him, his unit and the United States Army.

The Whole Person Concept

During the post-9/11 era, the vast majority of special operators have spent the majority of their time in environments full of chaos, danger, uncertainty, and unpredictability. When they aren't actually in such environments, they are typically participating in individual and unit training that is often designed to replicate real-world environments as closely as possible in preparation to once again deploy to a combat zone. This type of fast-paced operational tempo requires these warriors to perform at peak performance over long periods of time, while maintaining the strong-willed mindset and unwavering mental toughness that is necessary for success on the battlefield.

After a few years, SOF leaders began to notice that the nearly-continuous cycle of training for and deploying to combat environments was resulting in various negative effects on the members of their units. Simply stated, a significant number of special operators were experiencing a notable degradation in various aspects of their mental and physical well-being; and this was having a negative impact on the overall combat-readiness and efficiency of their units.

To remedy this situation, SOF leaders began to pay more attention to the "whole person" concept of training and preparing special operators to cope with the demands of repeated and intense training and deployment cycles. Before long, it became apparent that their efforts were yielding positive results, which led to the implementation of various training and educational programs and methods aimed at ensuring special operators are taking the right steps to ensure their health and well-being in all aspects of their personal and professional lives.

I believe that almost everyone that reads this book will acknowledge after reading this chapter that they need to increase their focus on one or more of the four main components that make up the "Whole Person" as described below. Don't be dispirited by finding that your "whole person" is imbalanced, admittedly many of the very highly-trained and physically and mentally tough members of SOF units were found to be lacking balance in their lives and needed to take action to refocus, rebalance, and in many aspects, revitalize various aspects of their lives.

The Whole Person Concept

The belief that a person's value to an organization derives strictly from his or her performance of tasks directly related to their job is a misconception that many people live under. Many feel that as long as they are delivering what is being asked of them, that is all that is necessary. Unfortunately many members of higher management in organizations hold this same belief. What results from this way of thinking are two equally negative outcomes: Unmotivated, uninspired, and initiative-lacking personnel; and, by default, inefficient, unproductive, and dysfunctional organizations, units, or teams.

The whole person concept refers to the development of an individual in all aspects and facets of their lives. An individual's life consists of more than just the work they do, both at work and at home; there's more to each individual than just their "job."

In developing yourself, as an individual, in order to be successful in achieving your goals, there are four aspects that you need to devote time and effort to:

The Mind

It is critical that you always aspire to increase your knowledge base through continuous learning. Whatever your job entails, you should at all times seek to learn more about it. Furthermore, you should strive to broaden your horizons on other topics as well. Any topic that you can read about or take a course on, that is related to your field, will probably bring forth ideas on things you can do, and inspire others to do, that will benefit your organization, team, or unit.

As you go through life you will discover hidden talents and skills that you excel at. It is imperative that you find a way to incorporate these into your "work" somehow. If that is not at all possible, then you should try to develop these outside of work in order to feel more fulfilled as a whole. The important thing to remember is that if you can tap into those talents you will benefit greatly, but also, just as important, you will help to create a more beneficial relationship with those around you, and accomplish greater results.

Special operators tend to be driven, life-long learners. What this means is that they are continuously striving to acquire new knowledge and capabilities. Whether it means mastering certain skills by learning quicker, better techniques, or learning new skills that will enhance their already acquired ones, they are in constant search of improvement. You'd be wise to follow their example and adopt a "continuous improvement" approach to your life!

The Body

In order to be able to stay focused and motivated at your job, you must be in good health. Unfortunately health and fitness are two areas that are greatly ignored by most people in their day-to-day lives. It seems that unless an individual is suffering from some illness, health is never a major focus. In order to be effective at what you do, you must have a healthy body. Without a healthy body, people tend to become lazy, demotivated, and ineffective.

Needless to say, SOF units require that all of their operators maintain very high levels of fitness. It is part of their everyday-life to incorporate a strict fitness regimen. But even if you don't work in a very physical environment, you should understand the benefits to a healthy lifestyle.

Health and fitness goes well beyond simply working out a few times a week. You must take into consideration nutrition, sleep habits, and rest and relaxation. If you neglect any one of these elements, whatever effort you put toward the others will be less fruitful. Make sure you take time to do some basic research and learn about proper nutrition and how it can greatly enhance almost every aspect of your life.

Likewise, you should make it a point to learn about what good sleep habits entail. It doesn't simply mean that you should sleep 8 hours per night; there are many elements that affect the quality of the sleep we are getting. Rest and relaxation doesn't just mean doing nothing for a period of time, it could mean doing more than you normally do, as long as it provides a respite from the every-day routine.

One thing is certain, when you adopt a healthier lifestyle, you will undoubtedly see an improvement in morale as well as productivity and efficiency. Not only will you feel better, more positive, but you will find that your daily tasks somehow seem easier to accomplish and reaching your goals will be less daunting.

The Heart

The heart is where your true passions live. The work you do for a living isn't always the work you are truly passionate about. It is when you find a way to implement your passion into your work that you will finally tap into your true potential. Your passion is what truly drives you. In my experience, it is crucial that you take control of your life and put your efforts toward finding the opportunity that will allow you to do what you truly love. The opportunity normally doesn't appear out of thin air, so don't just sit around waiting for it to come to you. Go out and make it happen!

The reason why most special operators are successful is because being an operator is their passion. It is something that lives deep down inside—it's a calling. They are able to subject themselves to the grueling training and the stressful lifestyle because they wake up each day knowing that they are truly "living the dream!"

You will find that once you have found a way to do what you love; your level of success will be significantly greater. When you're passionate about what you're doing the possibilities will be limitless and your accomplishments boundless!

The Spirit

Your inner core is your spirit. It is what guides you and leads you. You will find that at the core of most people is a desire to inspire others and to give of themselves to others. There are many ways to feed your spirit, but one of the most prevalent ones is to do good deeds for others. Whether this means volunteering for an organization that brings aid to the needy, or simply by finding one person whom you can help with a task, any way that you can be of "service" to another being will give you a sense of meaning and fulfillment.

There are some organizations that require you to do a certain number of hours of community service. However, when you comply with this requirement out of obligation rather than a desire to serve, it defeats the purpose. I would encourage you to find activities to be involved with that truly give you a sense of meaning. If you're passionate about children, you can volunteer for an organization that helps kids in tough situations. If you're passionate about animals, donate some of your time at an animal shelter.

The spirit is where you decipher whether or not through your passion, your true gifts and talents, and your service, you are truly creating and distributing value to others.

The Whole Person

To achieve significant strides in your personal growth, it is imperative that you understand this concept and endeavor to develop each of the 4 elements in yourself. Once you begin to do that, you will be well on your journey toward achieving the high levels of mental toughness you are seeking. An added benefit to implementing this concept within yourself, is the fact that helping others to achieve the same will become a habit.

True greatness comes from learning and getting to know yourself. This self-knowledge quickly opens your eyes to your true potential and strengthens your determination. Coupled with the other tools presented to you in this book, this concept has the power to make you unstoppable. So, don't wait, get off the sidelines and just get in the game. The only person stopping you is you!

Petty Officer Michael A. Monsoor
U.S. Navy SEAL

On September 29, 2006, in southern Ramadi, Iraq, Navy SEAL Michael Monsoor was assigned to serve as automatic weapons gunner in a combined SEAL and Iraqi Army sniper overwatch element positioned on a residential rooftop in a violent sector and historical stronghold for insurgents. His job was to protect the snipers.

Using tactical periscopes to scan over the walls for enemy activity, they soon spotted a group of four armed insurgents conducting reconnaissance for follow-on attacks of the U.S./Iraqi ground force moving through the area. The snipers killed one and wounded the other. Soon another enemy fighter was killed by snipers. The local supporters of the insurgents started blocking off the area around Monsoor's position in order to isolate their location for an attack.

The first attack occurred in the early afternoon, when a vehicle loaded with armed insurgents charged their position. Though the SEALs and Iraqis successfully repulsed the assault, they knew the insurgents would follow up with additional attacks. Despite this risk, the men stayed with the mission and refused to evacuate.

Monsoor, with his heavy machine-gun, was repositioned to the area right next to the door of the sniper nest on the roof outcrop that overlooked the most likely avenue of attack. As he surveyed the area for enemy movement, an insurgent was able to get close enough to throw a grenade onto their position. The grenade hit Monsoor on the chest and bounced onto the rooftop.

Despite the fact that Monsoor was standing right by the door and could have easily leapt to safety, he instead shouted "Grenade!" and jumped on top of it. The two SEALs closest to him escaped with only shrapnel wounds. Monsoor, however, having absorbed the majority of the blast was fatally wounded. The other 3 SEALs and 8 Iraqi soldiers survived. Although Monsoor was still alive when he arrived at the field hospital, he died from his wounds a few minutes later.

On April 8, 2008, Petty Officer Michael A. Monsoor was posthumously awarded the Medal of Honor, America's highest award for battlefield courage.

CITATION:

For conspicuous gallantry and intrepidity at the risk of his life above and beyond the call of duty while serving as Automatic Weapons Gunner in SEAL Team 3, Naval Special Warfare Task Group Arabian Peninsula, in support of Operation IRAQI FREEDOM on 29 September 2006. As a member of a combined SEAL and Iraqi Army sniper overwatch element, tasked with providing early warning and stand-off protection from a rooftop in an insurgent-held sector of Ar Ramadi, Iraq, Petty Officer Monsoor distinguished himself by his exceptional bravery in the face of grave danger. In the early morning, insurgents prepared to execute a coordinated attack by reconnoitering the area around the element's position. Element snipers thwarted the enemy's initial attempt by eliminating two insurgents. The enemy continued to assault the element, engaging them with a rocket-propelled grenade and small arms fire. As enemy activity increased, Petty Officer Monsoor took position with his machine gun between two teammates on an outcropping of the roof. While the SEALs vigilantly watched for enemy activity, an insurgent threw a hand grenade from an unseen location, which bounced off Petty Officer Monsoor's chest and landed in front of him. Although only he could have escaped the blast, Petty Officer Monsoor chose instead to protect his teammates. Instantly and without regard for his own safety, he threw himself onto the grenade to absorb the force of the explosion with his body, saving the lives of his two teammates. By his undaunted courage, fighting spirit, and unwavering devotion to duty in the face of certain death, Petty Officer Monsoor gallantly gave his life for his country, thereby reflecting great credit upon himself and upholding the highest traditions of the United States Naval Service.

Preparation and Practice

The basis of mental toughness lies on the confidence that an individual has in his or her unwavering faith in their ability to perform. This confidence in one's competence or skill is attained through training and practice—the type of practice that is conducted purposely and diligently in order to reach a mastery level of competence.

In *The Little Book of Talent*, author Dan Coyle emphasizes his belief that repetition is the key to mastery:

> *Repetition has a bad reputation. We tend to think of it as dull and uninspiring. But this perception is titanically wrong. Repetition is the single most powerful lever we have to improve skills, because it uses the built-in mechanism for making the wires of our brains faster and more accurate.*

I have no doubt that the vast majority of special operators would agree with Dan. Throughout their many years of challenging training, these men have learned that mastery of most of the skills associated with their roles is gained only through countless repetition in a variety of conditions, scenarios, and environments.

Dr. Anders Ericsson, a renowned expert in the field of high performance has conducted countless studies into what elements are necessary in order to reach expert-level skills. He has deduced that the key factor is a person's discipline in engaging in what he calls "deliberate practice."

Ericsson believes that there is a misconception regarding the origin of a person's abilities. For many years people held to the belief that anyone who reached high levels of expertise had innate qualities that allowed them to reach those heights, and that no normal human being could ever equal their achievements. Ericsson has long held that, aside from very few genetic differences such as height, there is no reason why any human being can't attain the same results. The key ingredient to becoming an expert performer is a life-long deliberate and constant pursuit of improvement.

Although top performers certainly possess qualities, traits, and habits that are the foundation of their success, none of these attributes are beyond the reach of any other human being. As mentioned in previous chapters, there are many incredibly gifted athletes who often fail to successfully complete SOF selection courses, while other far less physically capable men manage to pass and go on to serve very successfully as special operators.

One of Dr. Ericsson's fundamental findings was that becoming an expert at any skill has less to do with how much practice a person engages in and more with the quality of practice he or she engages in. He found that one way that differentiates the quality of the type of practice high performers engage in is that they concentrate on one specific skill at a time until it's perfected, then they move on to another one, and so on. Furthermore, each skill is practiced under a variety of realistic and increasingly challenging conditions.

The findings of Dr. Ericsson's research align with the overall attitude and approach used by members of all SOF units. To become good at something, you have to practice it, and practicing it perfectly under varying degrees of difficulty is a sure path to exceptional performance.

The knowledge gained from Dr. Ericsson's research should serve to galvanize individuals seeking to reach the top tiers of performance. It should remove anyone's doubt about his or her ability to become a high performer. All that is needed in order to attain your goals is the desire and the willingness to commit to painstaking practice and hard work.

When you practice a skill in the same stress-inducing scenarios and environments as when you "play," you will notice that when the time comes to perform a skill or action in real-life situations, you will be prepared—mentally and physically—and your performance won't be compromised.

As an example, SOF units are often required to engage in Close Quarter Battle (CQB) operations, which entail moving through a building inhabited by combatants as well as civilians. Their goal is to clear each room of enemy combatants, while making sure no civilians are harmed in the process. This type of mission requires an extraordinary level of proficiency in weapons handling.

In order to achieve this level of competence and proficiency, special operators assigned to assault units are required to practice CQB relentlessly. They focus on perfect practice, and this typically leads to perfect or near-perfect shooting. This kind of practice creates a form of muscle memory, and their brains begins to recognize various physical and mental patterns, which promotes faster and more efficient movement and clarity of thought over time.

Throughout my life I have applied the principle of perfect practice to most goals of great significance. I learned over time that the key to continuous high performance is continuous perfect practice. Below are some actions you can take that will benefit you greatly:

- **Reading.** The wealth of information that exists at our finger tips on just about any topic is immeasurable. You can find a book, article, or study on most topics by conducting a simple search on the web. By seeking out information on a topic of interest you will be able to acquire access to lessons learned by others and will significantly enhance your ability to rapidly elevate your level of performance. Reading about the experiences of others can help you avoid making the same mistakes they made. The vast majority of special operators I've ever known had an almost insatiable thirst for knowledge that was only quenched by constant reading. There's an old saying: "Experience is the best teacher, but it is also the most expensive!" I cannot emphasize this too strongly: *START READING NOW!*

- **Learning from the best.** Those who have already achieved a goal you may have set for yourself can be a very useful resource. The more you can learn from their background, education, and experience, the easier your path will be. Determine whether there are any traits, characteristics, and skills that you have in common with these top performers. There are probably many insights you can gain by observing them while they perform a task you are trying to improve upon. During my military career I learned a lot by interacting with members of U.S. and foreign special operations units. I found that almost all top-level performers in these units were very willing to share their experiences and advice with others. I encourage you to consider approaching someone you admire and asking them for advice and guidance.

- **Seeking feedback from the experts.** Ask a knowledgeable, competent person to observe you while you practice or perform, and ask them to provide you with honest, unvarnished feedback. It is important that you ask for feedback from those who will be honest with you and will tell you what you are doing well, what you are doing poorly, and what you should do in order to elevate your game. Don't take their feedback personally, but rather be open to criticism and advice and be ready to take action to correct your flaws.

- **Focus on winning.** Don't allow your fear of failure to overwhelm you. It will weaken your determination and have a very damaging effect on your confidence. Any candidate who goes into a SOF selection course thinking that he won't make it ... simply *doesn't make it!* The candidates who conclude the course standing tall on graduation day are those who entered the course with the unswerving belief that they had what it takes to make it and an *"I will die before I quit"* mentality.

If you anticipate mistakes and unexpected situations you will be better able to deal with them. Never allow the fear of losing or failing to perform dominate you—*THINK LIKE A WINNER!*

You can attain any goal you set your mind to as long as you are committed and willing to apply the concept of deliberate practice. It will require a significant investment of time, energy, and hard work, but when you reach the high level of performance you are seeking, it will all be worth it.

Four Levels of Competence

Now that you have been introduced to some of the methods for increasing mental toughness and have given some thought to how this quality is essential to reaching your goals, you are aware that you will probably need to learn some new skills (or enhance existing ones) in order to attain them. At this time it would be beneficial for you to be presented with some perspective about learning and competence.

A famous psychologist named Abraham Maslow introduced the concept that learning is made up of four levels. Although some may argue that this concept was developed by others working in the field of clinical psychology and the disciplines related to human behavior and training. Eventually this concept came to be known as the "Four Levels of Competence."

The essence of this concept entails understanding that at first glance individuals are unaware of their lack of knowledge in a specific topic. However as they become aware of this lack of knowledge, they recognize the need to focus on targeting their incompetence by acquiring the knowledge and skills to become competent. Once a level of competence is reached, individuals seek to increase their competence through continued practice in order to refine these skills. Eventually, the goal is to be able to "automatically" perform the action or skill without the need to deliberately think about how to execute it.

For the sake of simplicity, I'll use CQB and the development of recently selected members of SOF units from relatively untrained novices into fully qualified and certified special operations "shooters" to explain the Four Levels of Competence concept.

Level 1: Unconscious Incompetence

When a candidate makes it through selection and moves on to his follow-on training courses, having read countless books and having had the opportunity to interact with veteran operators, they fully believe that they know what being a special operator entails and that they are completely ready for the task. The reality is that they remain unaware of just how much training and practice is required before you are fully qualified to operate in real-world operations. They are, at that point, at the level of unconscious incompetence (UI). They simply "don't know what they don't know." Until they are well into their immersion into the CQB curriculum, they will have no idea of just how much more they have yet to learn.

During their follow-on training, operators will be exposed to sophisticated weapons, communications, and other highly technical equipment, and learn how to orchestrate it all into an effective plan of attack. And although they may have been introduced to certain aspects of CQB in their prior military training, they still have yet to be exposed to the more sophisticated and challenging stages of training and evaluation on this critical skill. Once they are, they quickly move from the unconscious incompetence level into the next stage of learning—conscious incompetence!

Level 2: Consciously Incompetent

At some point during the CQB training, the students realize that they have been unaware of the many primary and secondary skills that are associated with becoming a fully qualified "shooter." Now conscious of their incompetence, they begin to understand that while they have learned how to operate a rifle and handgun, they aren't even close to meeting the minimum standards that they will have to meet in order to become fully qualified shooters.

Even after graduation from the operator training course and reporting into their first operational unit, these newly designated operators will remain in the consciously incompetent group for quite some time as they are exposed to additional training and execute countless CQB drills and graded live-fire exercises. Aware that they still lack a high-level of competence in some aspects of shooting, they willingly seek help in acquiring mastery of these skills. Typically, these new operators become highly motivated "students of the gun" and become determined to learn and do whatever is necessary to become fully qualified and accepted by their more experienced teammates.

Level 3: Consciously Competent

Through exposure to proper training and continuous deliberate practice as well as very detailed, individual coaching, these operators begin to develop true competence. The arduous training they receive manifests in their ability to demonstrate their ability to "shoot to standard" under a variety of conditions and during exercises and scenarios of ever increasing difficulty.

The speed and accuracy that once seemed difficult or perhaps even impossible now seems much more attainable. Their movement through the dark hallways and rooms of the shooting houses becomes more fluid and efficient. Reloading and clearing of weapon malfunctions becomes almost effortless, as does the transition from rifle to pistol when the situation requires it. Decisions regarding "friend or foe" and "shoot/don't shoot" are made much more quickly; and they begin to develop as solid members of an assault team.

Despite this new level of competence, however, these operators still need to consciously think about almost every action they are performing. At this point, every decision and action is the result of an intricate thought process and these men have not yet reached a "reflex response." They are still not ready for real-world CQB operations that require split second, reflex-driven decisions. Only with continued practice under realistic and demanding conditions can they cross into the unconsciously competent stage.

Level 4: Unconsciously Competent

The final and ultimate stage of competence implies that the shooters have, after performing thousands of repetitions of various CQB skills and techniques, literally programmed their minds and bodies to react and execute without any perceivable thought or deliberation. At this level of competence, the shooters can move rapidly through a building and clearing it of enemy forces by capturing or killing them. When the operation is completed, they often realize that they changed the magazines in their weapon once or twice during the assault, yet they have little or no memory of doing so.

They are now able to perform flawlessly during very stressful and dynamic situations because their extensive training overrides their conscious thought processes. Individually, and as a team, they can now execute at the level of speed, precision and accuracy that is required during missions that involving a variety of scenarios, such as the high-profile operation in which operators from SEAL Team Six killed the notorious Al Qaeda leader, Osama bin Laden.

An example of this phenomenon of Unconscious Competence can best be described by the account of how Navy SEAL Senior Chief Matt Dale was able to survive an "arms-length" CQB encounter during a direct-action mission in Iraq. This anecdote is taken from the book *The Sheriff of Ramadi* by retired Navy SEAL Captain Dick Couch:

> On this day Senior Chief Dale needed all of that and more.
>
> The three insurgents focused their attention and guns on Matt Dale. One of their initial bursts took off part of his thumb and knocked away his rifle. As he had done so often in simulation, Chief Dale reached for the pistol on his hip, a Sig Saur 9mm, and brought the weapon level. Then he began to shoot: sight picture and squeeze, sight picture and squeeze, sight picture and squeeze. While Dale was shooting them, they were shooting him. The Senior Chief was hit an astonishing twenty-seven times. Eleven of those rounds were stopped by his body armor. Sixteen of those rounds went through him. 'It was easier to say where I wasn't hit than where I was hit.' But when it was over, three insurgents lay dead and Matt Dale was still standing.
>
> 'I didn't have time to think about it,' Chief Dale told me, 'My primary (weapon) was gone before I got a round off. The rest was instinct and training. I knew I had to get my pistol and there it was, in my hand and I was shooting.' I asked him what he was thinking—was

feeling. 'Pure anger,' he said. 'I don't remember much other than I was incredibly pissed off—that they had shot away my rifle and that they were shooting at me. I guess I was able to focus all my anger on the insurgents and stay in the fight. I didn't stop shooting until the slide locked and they were all down.'

Your Journey through the Four Levels of Competence

I have no doubt that you will progress through the Four Levels of competence as you pursue your goals, whatever they may be. This is especially true if your goals are exceptionally challenging or if they are associated with tasks, skills or topics in which you have little or no experience. Remember, all special operators, including those on the bin Laden raid and other high-profile missions that have been recently disclosed to the public, were once at the Unconscious Incompetence level. Likewise, as new members of a SOF unit, very few of them had any awareness that some of the specialized tactics, techniques, equipment and technology routinely utilized even existed!

The point is that all high-achievers, including those who have already achieved what you may aspire to accomplish, were once beginners and didn't possess the knowledge, skills, and competence required to achieve great things.

Upon achieving competence, you will soon realize that it doesn't end there. You will inevitably see that all the hard work you did to become competent in a skill will all be in vain if you don't do the work to remain competent. Remember that most professional arenas are very dynamic and technologies are constantly changing and being upgraded. So whether you are trying to learn a new skill for work, attain a weight-loss goal, become a better salesman, or learn a new medical technique, you must continue deliberately practicing and trying to constantly improve upon it. All your hard work, patience and continuous deliberate practice will lead you to achieving success.

Setting Goals

A research study conducted by Dr. David Kohl, professor emeritus at Virginia Tech, revealed that 80% of Americans don't have goals. Sixteen percent do have goals, but fail to record them in some way so they can be reviewed and their progress assessed. Three percent do have a written list of goals, but they don't review them on a regular basis. Only one percent, the highest achievers, establish clearly defined goals, write them down and review them on an on-going basis.

In the book *Mind Gym, An Athlete's Guide to Inner Excellence*, sports psychologist Gary Mack stated that:

> *Goal setting is a master skill for personal growth and peak performance. I can't stress this too much. Without goals, where will you go in life? If you don't know where you are headed, you're probably going to wind up somewhere other than where you want to be. . . . I encourage athletes to set daily or short-term goals. The way to achieve long-term goals is to break them down into small steps. Effective goal setting is like a*

staircase. Each step is an action step—an increment of progress. The old saying is 'Inch by inch it's a cinch.'

As you forge ahead on your journey toward self-improvement and enhancing mental toughness, you will see that everything that you wish to accomplish hinges upon your ability to effectively establish and plan out your goals. Every major accomplishment is the product of a carefully charted vision. In order to reach your ultimate objective, you must learn how to structure your plan of attack so that your vision will be realized.

The SMART Goal Technique

There are countless goal setting techniques, one of the most popular ones is called the SMART goal setting method. The S M A R T stands for: Specific, Measurable, Attainable, Relevant, and Time-bound. By using this method you will integrate the ability to track your progress and verify that the course you are on will lead you to success. You will be able to define milestones and assess the goal's attainability along the way.

A senior enlisted leader assigned to an Air Force special operations unit had this to say about goal setting:

Goal setting involves setting your own performance objectives with a clear plan for how you will achieve them. Setting long-term goals keeps you focused on the big picture, while short and mid-term goals guide and motivate you over time.

Goals should also be Specific, Measurable, Achievable, Relevant, and Time-sensitive. Specific goals are clear and well-defined and can often be framed by answering the five 'Ws'...who, what, when, where and why. Having measurable goals prevents frustration or burnout because you are able to assess progress over time. Goals should also be relevant and time-sensitive.

An example of a SMART goal might be: 'In order to improve my physical fitness, I will swim 1,000 meters in less than 20 minutes within 16 weeks,' while that broader plan will likely require smaller segmented goals in order to truly be achievable.

Goal setting is critical to most any successful endeavor because it helps to focus your attention, prioritize efforts, enhance persistence, and develop effective learning strategies. Otherwise, suboptimal performance or outright failure is more likely as the person procrastinates or simply flies by the seat of their pants without a viable plan.

A highly experienced Navy SEAL leader shared his thoughts on goal setting:

During BUD/S, students learn to 'chunk' each mission into manageable goals. For instance, your aim could be to survive to lunchtime. Once you do that, you pat yourself on the back, refocus, and set the next goal: Make it to dinner. SEALs also apply the principle of chunking to tactical planning and basically any tasks they are assigned by evaluating if they are 'specific, measurable, attainable, realistic, and timely—or SMART. This approach can apply to any goal, whether it involves fitness, relationships, or work. Eventually, goal setting becomes second-nature. You're constantly seeking ways to improve every aspect of your performance.

Let's learn more about the five elements of the SMART goal technique!

Specific Goals

Rather than focusing your efforts blindly trekking toward a vague, overly broad goal or objective, you should take the time to clearly and succinctly define your goals. It is important that you write out exactly what it is that you wish to accomplish. Keep in mind that specific goals can be part of a larger plan or objective. In order for a goal to fit into the "specific" category, you can ask the following questions, and if you can answer each of them easily, then you have a good level of specificity:

What is it that I want to accomplish?

When does it need to happen?

Who needs to be involved?

Where do I need to be physically in order to make it happen?

How can I make this happen?

Why is it necessary?

Measurable Goals

In order to ensure that your goals can be achieved and your ultimate objective realized you must put in place criteria that can be used for measuring progress. Having some kind of tracking mechanism will help you stay on track, and will make it easier to adjust your plan, should unforeseen obstacles arise. Measurable goals can also go a long way in refining what exactly it is that you want to accomplish and whether your objective is attainable.

To make a goal measurable you will need to have concrete evidence to mark your progress. Timelines are a good way to be able to see and measure any strides you're making toward your goals. For example, you can set target dates defining when a deliverable outcome should happen. You must define what your desired end-state is in order to know when you have accomplished what you set out to do.

Attainable Goals

As you go through this process, each step will help you decide whether your goals are actually reachable. Your must weigh the effort, time, energy, people, and money that may be involved in reaching your goals, if any of these factors is insufficient, then you need to redefine your goals. It is a futile exercise to set goals that are unrealistic, it will make the task seem too daunting and will ensure failure before you even begin.

Don't misunderstand what I'm trying to say. I'm not trying to talk you out of setting challenging goals that will require extreme effort and mental fortitude. On the contrary, the point of this chapter is to provide you with a method that you can use as a tool that will aid you in achieving those higher-level, more complex objectives.

A good method is to simplify your objectives into smaller pieces that will bring you closer to achieving grander, loftier ones. As you reach these "micro-goals," your self-confidence, skills, and abilities will increase. Goals that seemed unreachable at one point will seem more attainable as your attitude and skills develop.

Relevant Goals

The relevance of the objective you are trying to reach must be taken into account. Depending on whether your goal is a personal one or a professional one will help you decide whether a goal is relevant. Can your ability to run a marathon affect whether you get promoted next quarter? Probably not. Make sure that you are setting goals that will truly impact what you wish to accomplish in the long term. You must ask yourself whether accomplishing this goal will get you closer to where you want to be.

Time-bound Goals

Having deadlines for accomplishing milestones will encourage you to prioritize your time and your actions. The sense of urgency that a deadline imposes on us tends to decrease the possibility of allowing external factors to delay our efforts. Furthermore, when "more pressing concerns" threaten to derail your timeline, being able to shift some deadlines will prevent you from losing momentum. It is important to allow some flexibility when setting your time limits and deadlines as it will maintain a good balance in morale and motivation. Being overly stringent on your timeline will have overall negative effects on your ability to accomplish your goals.

As stated previously, self-confidence and mental toughness are two major elements that affect your ability to accomplish your goals. When you have set your eyes on an objective, the challenges that you face when trying to attain it will require a great deal of resiliency, will power, and discipline. However, as beneficial as acquiring the qualities that increase your mental toughness could be, that effort won't yield optimal results if the goals and objectives themselves are not well thought out and clearly defined.

The SMART goal setting process will enable you to chart out a concise, detailed plan that will ensure your ability to accomplish your objective. This is a tried and true method that has been implemented by countless SOF operators throughout their careers, it has yielded very positive results for professionals in the business world, athletes, and members of the medical field, it has worded for me, and it will definitely work for you.

There is an old adage you have probably heard at some point in your life: "If you fail to plan, you are planning to fail!" These are words to live by indeed!

Take Action

If you study high-achievers, in any aspect of life, you'll find that their approach to achieving significant and challenging goals typically revolves around a belief that says: "I can do this if I am willing to pay the price." Author Scott Adams says the same thing in his book titled *How to Fail at Almost Everything and Still Win Big*:

> One of the best pieces of advice I've ever heard goes something like this: If you want success, figure out the price, then pay it. It sounds trivial and obvious, but if you unpack the idea it has extraordinary power. I know a lot of people who wish they were rich or famous or otherwise fabulous. They wish they had yachts and servants and castles and they wish they could travel the world in their own private jets. But these are mere wishes. Few of these wishful people have decided to have any of the things they wish for. It's a key difference, for once you decide, you take action. Wishing starts in the mind and generally stays there. When you decide to be

successful in a big way, it means you acknowledge the
price and you're willing to pay it.

Reflect for a moment on what you've just read and how it applies to you.

What do YOU want?

Do you believe you can have it?

What price will you need to pay?

And most importantly, are you willing to pay it?

With the information that has been presented thus far in the book, you are now equipped with some basic knowledge and strategies for developing or increasing your mental toughness and self-confidence. If you adopt these same techniques and thought processes, you too can develop the ability to perform well in the most challenging situations, and will be well on your way to achieving the goals you have set.

Clarity of Goals

Having clearly defined goals will enable you to be able to break them down into carefully thought-out micro-tasks. Tracking your progress will give you a sense of accomplishment and keep you motivated; it will also ensure that you will reach success in a timely manner. You can use the SMART Goals Method (although there are many other goal-setting techniques that you can research and use) to chart out a detailed plan that will ensure an efficient path to reaching your goals.

Preparation and Practice

It is important that you understand what "practice" truly entails. Simply going through the motions of a skill or task will not yield the results necessary for elevated proficiency and success. This is achieved only through constant, realistic, and challenging practice sessions that replicate the actual "game day" conditions as much as possible, taking into consideration factors that might affect your performance and being ready to respond effectively to them.

Rehearsal is a very efficient tool when dealing with situations or activities—job interviews, executive briefings, oral presentations, music recitals, etc.—that often cause anxiety. It is important to take the time and find different ways to expose yourself to the element that causes you anxiety, and force yourself to perform in that environment.

Confidence

Self-confidence results from taking the time, putting in the effort, and making the decision to use the tools presented in this book to attain a goal or achieve a dream. Taking on the challenge to achieve a specific goal, along with the will power to work relentlessly until it is achieved, regardless of any obstacles that arise along the way, are the qualities that distinguish high-achieving, successful people.

Controlling Fear

The human body is programmed to respond to dangerous and stressful situations in predictable ways that can have a negative impact on performance. These can be neutralized by utilizing the Seven Pillar Technique and other techniques and concepts mentioned throughout this book. Controlling fear and stress is a learned skill, and one that must be practiced and honed into sharpness. Try to do so at every opportunity, especially when engaged in activities that are directly related to the achievement of your most important and challenging goals.

Controlling Your Thoughts

Mental toughness is, in essence, your ability to exert control—with your mind—over your thoughts, your actions, your decisions, your body, and yourself. It involves having the strength of will and the power to influence your attitude, not allowing negativity to take over and drain you of your energy and motivation. Controlling your thoughts will enable you to keep your sights on your goals rather than on the obstacles in your way, while at the same time remaining positive and motivated.

Putting It All Together

All the concepts presented in this book will aid you in increasing your levels of mental toughness and self-confidence. The changes you will experience once you've put them into practice will be noticeable not only to you, but to everyone around you. This newly gained level of confidence will manifest in various ways: The self-assured way you carry yourself, how eloquently you speak, and your overall positive and enthusiastic demeanor. One thing is certain; putting these elements into effect can monumentally enhance your efficiency and catapult you to new heights of achievement!

Conclusion

In this book, I did my best to summarize some of the qualities that comprise the foundation of America's elite units' winning mindset. I attempted to paint a picture of their methodology—how they think and how they approach various situations and tasks, and the reasons why. You should now realize that even though these warriors are truly special men, what makes them exceptional is not their physical strength or specific warrior skills; it is the steely, unbreachable will that resides in their minds that truly sets them apart from most people.

I have included examples depicting how special operators have unyieldingly persevered under unfathomable, dire circumstances that would cause most others to simply quit and surrender to the situation facing them. You should close this book knowing that the mental toughness, self-confidence and other traits and qualities demonstrated by these exceptional warriors are attainable by anyone who desires to have them and has the initiative to put them into action.

Aware that you already possess the necessary talent and aptitude to achieve your goals, you should now gain access to any and all individuals and resources that can help you get started on your journey to success. No more time for inspirational and motivating stories—it is time for YOU to take action!

Good Luck!

Made in the USA
Monee, IL
11 May 2023